P9-CEZ-865

THE
HARVARD MEDICAL
SCHOOL GUIDE TO
LOWERING YOUR

BLOOD PRESSURE

Also from McGraw-Hill and Harvard Medical School

Living Through Breast Cancer, by Carolyn M. Kaelin, M.D., M.P.H., with Francesca Coltrera

Eat, Play, and Be Healthy, by W. Allan Walker, M.D., with Courtney Humphries

Beating Diabetes, by David M. Nathan, M.D., and Linda M. Delahanty, M.S., R.D.

Lowering Your Cholesterol, by Mason W. Freeman, M.D., with Christine Junge

Healing Your Sinuses, by Ralph B. Metson, M.D., with Steven Mardon

Achieving Optimal Memory, by Aaron P. Nelson, Ph.D., with Susan Gilbert

Overcoming Thyroid Problems, by Jeffrey R. Garber, M.D., with Sandra Sardella White

The No Sweat Exercise Plan, by Harvey B. Simon, M.D.

Raising an Emotionally Healthy Child When a Parent Is Sick, by Paula K. Rauch, M.D., and Anna C. Muriel, M.D., M.P.H.

THE

HARVARD MEDICAL

SCHOOL GUIDE TO

LOWERING YOUR

BLOOD PRESSURE

AGGIE CASEY, R.N., M.S., AND

HERBERT BENSON, M.D.

WITH **BRIAN O'NEILL**

McGraw·Hill

New York   Chicago   San Francisco   Lisbon   London   Madrid   Mexico City
Milan   New Delhi   San Juan   Seoul   Singapore   Sydney   Toronto

The McGraw·Hill Companies

Library of Congress Cataloging-in-Publication Data

Casey, Aggie.
    The Harvard Medical School guide to lowering your blood pressure / by Aggie Casey and Herbert Benson, with Brian O'Neill.
        p.   cm.
    Includes index.
    ISBN 0-07-144801-2
    1. Hypertension.   2. Hypertension—Treatment.   I. Benson, Herbert, 1935– .
II. O'Neill, Brian E.   III. Harvard Medical School.   IV. Title.

RC685.H8.C37   2006
616.1'32—dc22   2005030161

Copyright © 2006 by the President and Fellows of Harvard College. All rights reserved. Printed in the United States of America. Except as permitted under the United States Copyright Act of 1976, no part of this publication may be reproduced or distributed in any form or by any means, or stored in a database or retrieval system, without the prior written permission of the publisher.

6 7 8 9 0 DIG/DIG   10

ISBN 0-07-144801-2

Interior design by Think Design Group, LLC

Artwork on pages 4, 11, 16 by Harriet Greenfield; page 28 by Scott Leighton; page 53 by Sebastien LeMenager; page 91 by Salvatore Familia

Grateful acknowledgment to Jim Huddleston, P.T., for writing Chapter 5, and to Narmin Virani, RD, for writing Chapter 4.

McGraw-Hill books are available at special quantity discounts to use as premiums and sales promotions, or for use in corporate training programs. For more information, please write to the Director of Special Sales, Professional Publishing, McGraw-Hill, Two Penn Plaza, New York, NY 10121-2298. Or contact your local bookstore.

The information contained in this book is intended to provide helpful and informative material on the subject addressed. It is not intended to serve as a replacement for professional medical advice. Any use of the information in this book is at the reader's discretion. The author, publisher, and the President and Fellows of Harvard College specifically disclaim any and all liability arising directly or indirectly from the use or application of any information contained in this book. A health care professional should be consulted regarding your specific situation.

This book is printed on acid-free paper.

I, Aggie Casey, dedicate this book to
my daughter, Ali Barros, and to
my husband, Charlie, for their continuous
love and support. I would also like to
thank my parents, Agnes and Bill Casey,
for believing in me. I love all of you
with my life.

I, Herbert Benson, am forever grateful to
my wife, Marilyn.

Contents

Acknowledgments

The information and advice offered in these pages reflect the integrated approach to patient care we practice at the Mind/Body Medical Institute (M/BMI) in Boston. We would like to acknowledge all of our colleagues at the M/BMI for their continued work in the field of mind/body medicine and for sharing their knowledge and expertise with us.

We would especially like to thank our esteemed colleagues and friends in the Cardiac Wellness Program at M/BMI, Jim Huddleston, Narmin Virani, Elizabeth Carrozza, and Sarah Lynch. Their passion to their work made our book a reality.

We offer warm thanks to Brian O'Neill for his guidance in researching medical literature and helping to write this book. In addition, we would like to thank our colleagues at Harvard Medical School for helping to make this book a reality: Anthony Komaroff, M.D., editor-in-chief at Harvard Health Publications; Edward Coburn, publishing director; and Nancy Ferrari, managing editor.

We would like to thank Judith McCarthy, our invaluable editor at McGraw-Hill, for giving us this opportunity.

Finally, we would like to thank our patients for their willingness to share their stories and for allowing us to be part of their journey toward optimal health.

Introduction

Patricia didn't feel or look sick. In fact, when the trim sixty-three-year-old mother of three adult children walked into my clinic in January 2005, she was the very picture of a healthy woman—healthier, even, than many people one-third her age. She ate a balanced diet, walked three miles three times a week, and was an avid golfer and cyclist. And having recently retired from a rewarding career as a seventh-grade teacher, she now spent her days with her husband of forty-two years in the beachside town of Chatham, Massachusetts.

But Patricia *did* need to be concerned about her health.

She had one of the most prevalent and most threatening diseases in our culture. The only problem was she wasn't suffering any symptoms, which is how this disease, operating with assassin-like stealth, has earned the name the "silent killer." The only reason she knew she needed to become concerned was that her blood pressure readings in her physician's office were higher than they once had been. Patricia had hypertension (high blood pressure).

You're probably reading this book because you or someone you love has been diagnosed with hypertension. You're not alone. If you're an American adult, there is an almost one-in-three chance that you will develop hypertension. The incidence of the disease has risen steadily since the 1960s, and now it is estimated that 96 million Americans have it.

Like most people, you probably never saw it coming. Take Patricia, who had long known that the key to avoiding hypertension was to refrain from smoking, get regular exercise, limit alcohol use, and eat a healthy diet. Yet here she was in my office. What had gone wrong?

She had three powerful forces working against her. The first had been with her from birth: her family history. In fact, one of the leading risk factors recognized today is a close relative who also has hypertension. Patricia's mother has hypertension and takes medication for the disease at age eighty-eight.

Second, Patricia identified significant family stress over the past few years. She frequently felt frustrated and unsure how to deal with these conflicts. Persistent, unmanaged stress is also a leading risk factor for developing hypertension.

Third was a recent change that raised Patricia's (and 45 million other Americans') risk with one simple announcement. For more than twenty years her blood pressure readings had been below 140/90 mm/Hg. She assumed her blood pressure was nothing to worry about, and her doctors had confirmed that assumption. In her own words, she didn't pay an awful lot of attention to it because she was within the guidelines of the time. Then all of that changed. In 2003 the Joint National Committee on Prevention, Detection, Evaluation, and Treatment of High Blood Pressure (JNC 7) reclassified blood pressures above 120–139/80–89 mm/Hg as a new category called *prehypertension*. Experts believe this new category more accurately reflects where risk associated with high blood pressure really begins. What risk? Hypertension triples the risk of dying of a heart attack and increases the risk of a stroke sevenfold over people with normal blood pressure.

If you or someone you love has been diagnosed with hypertension, you probably want to understand the challenges that may lie ahead. But most of all, you're wondering what to do next. That's why we wrote this book. The Mind/Body Medical Institute (M/BMI) has helped thousands of patients like Patricia to lower their blood pressure, often without the use of medication.

M/BMI evolved from more than thirty years of pioneering work in the field of mind/body medicine by Herbert Benson, M.D., and his colleagues at Harvard Medical School. The relaxation response, as described by Dr. Benson in his 1975 bestselling book of the same title, is the foundation of mind/body medicine as practiced at the Institute, in conjunction with nutrition, exercise, and stress management.

Many people with hypertension and many doctors shrug off the importance of lifestyle changes, and that's too bad. Losing weight, exercising more, eating better, and learning to elicit the relaxation response can all lead to fundamental physical changes that go far beyond improving blood pressure. They also chip away at high blood sugar and high cholesterol, improve artery flexibility, and improve your physical and emotional health. No pill or combination of pills can match this.

When Patricia finished our thirteen-week lifestyle modification program, which included supervised exercise, nutrition counseling, and stress management, she had not only lowered her blood pressure to a healthy reading of 111/78 mm/Hg, but also found, as you will, that the mind/body techniques she learned had crossed over into other parts of her life.

This book is for anybody who wants to learn how to lower his or her blood pressure. And the good news is you *can* learn how.

We'll start with a user's tour of the circulatory system and learn why the two numbers that make up your blood pressure measurement are so important. Next we will talk about lifestyle modification, including stress management, healthier eating, and physical activity. Finally, we'll pull it all together into a program that's not only simple to follow and fun to do, but that also improves total quality of life and well-being. Your heart and arteries will thank you, as will the friends and loved ones who know that you have taken charge of your future for a life of health and wellness. You can't change your family history, but you can change your approach to healthful living. It worked for Patricia, as it has for countless others, and it can work for you too.

And so, if you are ready, let's begin.

THE
HARVARD MEDICAL
SCHOOL GUIDE TO
LOWERING YOUR
BLOOD PRESSURE

CHAPTER 1

Understanding Hypertension

The fact that you're reading the words on this page means that hypertension has somehow touched your life. Maybe a spouse or parent has recently been diagnosed with it. Maybe you've been told that you're at risk and want to explore your options. Or maybe you have just been diagnosed. When hypertension touches someone's life—as it does in some way for almost all Americans—it can be frustrating, scary, and confusing. This book is about adopting a lifestyle modification program aimed at lowering your blood pressure. In order to do that, you should understand just what blood pressure is, what the term *high blood pressure* means, and why it's a cause for concern. This chapter is designed to lay the foundation for the lifestyle program that follows. We'll cover blood pressure basics and the different types of hypertension.

Hypertension: An Important Update

Imagine going to bed one evening thinking you had a perfectly normal blood pressure, only to wake up the next morning and discover that it had entered the danger zone. That's exactly what happened to 45 million Americans in the spring of 2003 when a new publication came out. What kind of publication could raise

FIGURE 1.1 Blood Pressure and Categories of Hypertension

<120/80	120/80–139/89	140/90–159/99	160+/100+
Normal	Prehypertension	Stage 1 hypertension	Stage 2 hypertension

45 million people's blood pressure? No, it wasn't a Stephen King novel or another book by Bill O'Reilly, but a report by the Joint National Committee on Prevention, Detection, Evaluation, and Treatment of High Blood Pressure (JNC 7). The committee announced new national guidelines that changed the definition of "normal" blood pressure.

All hypertension is high blood pressure, but not all high blood pressure is hypertension. The term *high blood pressure* covers any blood pressure above 120/80 mm/Hg, while *hypertension* refers only to pressures of 140/90 mm/Hg and above. (For people with diabetes, high blood pressure is 130/80 mm/Hg.) What's more, hypertension is divided into three levels of acuteness—prehypertension, stage I hypertension, and stage II hypertension—as shown in Figure 1.1.

Under the former guidelines, published in 1997, your blood pressure was considered normal if your systolic pressure was under 140 mm/Hg and your diastolic pressure was under 90 mm/Hg. (In that classification, "normal" meant usual or average. It didn't, contrary to popular opinion, mean "healthy.") The new guidelines classified systolic pressures of 120–139 mm/Hg or diastolic pressures of 80–89 mm/Hg as a new category of high blood pressure called *prehypertension*. This means that a person's blood pressure hasn't crossed the official hypertension threshold, but it likely will over time unless corrective actions are taken.

Blood Pressure Basics

Performing under pressure is what your arteries were designed to do best. Though you can't see it or feel it, inside your body at this moment and at every moment of every day your heart and arteries are involved in a complex rhythm of pressure and resistance. Blood pressure is the amount of force exerted by the blood on the inside of your arteries as the blood is pumped throughout your circulatory system. Each time your heart muscle contracts, blood is pressed against the walls of the arteries and is measured as systolic blood pressure (the top number). When the heart relaxes between beats, the pressure on the artery wall eases, measured as diastolic blood pressure (the bottom number).

Your blood pressure is never constant, nor should it be. Your body continuously adjusts to the daily demands placed on it. It can make dramatic adjustments in blood pressure within seconds. A sprint for the elevator, the sound of breaking glass, or a confrontation with someone may send blood pressure soaring from an idling 130/70 mm/Hg to a racing 160/100 mm/Hg or higher.

Understanding the Numbers

No doubt you have had your blood pressure measured countless times. In fact, it has probably been taken every time you've visited your doctor. When your doctor tightens an inflatable cuff around your upper arm and places a stethoscope at your inner elbow (as shown in Figure 1.2), he or she is about to get a peek into the workings of your circulatory system. The cuff is inflated with air to compress the brachial artery, the major artery in the arm. The cuff is first inflated to a pressure that shuts off all blood flow to the artery. As the cuff is slowly deflated, your doctor listens (through a stethoscope placed on the artery) for two things. First, he or she will hear the sound of blood rushing back into the compressed artery, and note this number on the gauge to determine the systolic blood pressure. As the pressure in the cuff continues to be released, your doctor listens for the moment where the sounds taper off and disappear. The number at which the last beat is audible indicates the diastolic blood pressure.

A typical blood pressure reading might look something like this: 120/80 mm/Hg. That means, in this instance, that the per-

FIGURE 1.2 Measuring Blood Pressure

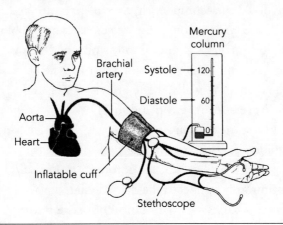

son's blood pressure is expressed as a systolic reading of 120 millimeters of mercury (Hg being the chemical symbol for mercury) and a diastolic reading of 80 millimeters of mercury. Most mercury blood pressure units have been phased out and newer nonmercury devices are readily available. Many modern instruments use a spring gauge with a round dial or a digital monitor, but even these are calibrated to give readings in mm/Hg.

An ideal blood pressure reading is 120/80 mm/Hg or lower. The higher the numbers go, the harder your heart is working to do its job. And your heart is working hard enough already. This remarkable ten-ounce muscle, about the size of your fist, beats nearly 100,000 times and circulates some 1,900 gallons of blood throughout your body each day. When the heart has to work overtime, the muscle can become enlarged, and the arteries, under the relentless pounding of the blood against the arterial walls, become rigid and narrow, potentially putting you at risk for stroke, kidney failure, and heart disease.

What the Readings Mean

You already know that the top number (systolic pressure) measures the force of blood against the arteries as the heart contracts and that the bottom number (diastolic pressure) measures arterial pressure when the heart relaxes between beats. Simply put, your blood pressure (BP) reading measures how hard your heart is working to pump blood throughout your body and also the condition of your arteries. The amount of blood that is pumped out of your heart is known as the *blood volume*, or *cardiac output* (CO). The resistance offered by the blood vessels as the blood is pumped is known as the *systemic vascular resistance* (SVR). Your blood pressure equals the amount of blood pumped out of your heart multiplied by the resistance it encounters from your arteries as it's being pumped throughout the body:

$$BP = CO \times SVR$$

As CO or SVR increase, so does BP. This is because in both cases, the heart must work harder to push the necessary amount of blood through the arteries.

Different Kinds, Varying Degrees

Just as there are varying degrees of hypertension, there are also different classifications, which we'll look at now.

Primary Hypertension

Physicians classify the different kinds of hypertension based on their causes and characteristics. Up to 95 percent of people with hypertension have what's called *primary hypertension*, or essential hypertension. This means the condition has no identifiable source. Most experts believe essential hypertension is caused by a variety of lifestyle factors, such as diet, exercise, and smoking. It is estimated that about 50 percent of the population is "salt sensitive," meaning that a high sodium intake will raise their blood pressure.

Secondary Hypertension

As its name implies, secondary hypertension arises from an underlying physical cause such as kidney disease or adrenal disorders.

Only about 5–10 percent of all cases of hypertension are from a secondary cause; here are some of the most common.

Renal Artery Stenosis. One cause of secondary hypertension is renal artery stenosis, the narrowing of an artery that supplies your kidneys with blood. This condition can occur as a result of plaque on the arterial wall or, in young women, from an overgrowth of muscular tissue in the arterial wall (fibromuscular dysplasia). Some cases require bypass surgery, but most can be treated successfully with angioplasty. This procedure dilates the constricted artery with an inflatable balloon that's attached to a catheter.

Hyperaldosteronism. Another cause of secondary hypertension is overproduction of aldosterone, the hormone made by the adrenal glands that helps your kidneys regulate potassium and sodium levels. This condition, called *hyperaldosteronism*, causes the body to retain sodium and lose potassium, leading to hypertension, weight gain, muscle weakness, and water retention. If a tumor in the adrenal gland is causing the overproduction, the usual treatment is surgery. In other cases, people with this condition need to restrict their salt intake and take a medication that blocks the action of aldosterone.

Hyperthyroidism. The thyroid is a gland located in your throat just in front of your windpipe; it produces hormones to regulate the way your body uses energy. When the thyroid becomes hyperactive, a condition known as *hyperthyroidism*, it overproduces hormones, leading to changes in heartbeat and blood pressure, in addition to changes in weight, digestion, and muscle function.

Pheochromocytoma. A rare, usually noncancerous tumor called a *pheochromocytoma* secretes excessive amounts of the hormones that regulate nervous system activity; this constricts most arteries and raises blood pressure. Other symptoms may include tremors, palpitations, sweating, nervousness, headache, weight loss, and fainting. Treatment consists of medications that block the hor-

White-Coat Hypertension

Stress can elevate blood pressure, and for this reason, some people whose blood pressure is usually normal may appear to have elevated levels in a medical situation such as a visit to the doctor's office. This phenomenon is dubbed *white-coat hypertension*. In the past, doctors often dismissed these elevated readings as a reflection of the temporary anxiety many people experience at the clinic or hospital. But now some experts think white-coat hypertension is worth investigating because it might shed light on how stress influences blood pressure. It is estimated that 15–30 percent of people with hypertension have white-coat hypertension.

mones' effects and surgery to remove the tumor. Pheochromocytomas are typically confined to the adrenal glands, which lie on top of the kidneys. However, about 10 percent spread beyond the adrenals or arise at other sites in the body. If a surgeon cannot remove the tumor, radiation or chemotherapy is necessary.

Labile Hypertension

Labile means "ever-changing," and in labile hypertension, blood pressure fluctuates far more than usual. Your blood pressure might soar from 119/76 mm/Hg at 10 A.M. to 170/104 mm/Hg at 4 P.M. These fluctuations can result from a variety of sources, such as too much caffeine, anxiety attacks, or stress overload. Whatever the cause, these transient episodes of hypertension may be dangerous and should be treated.

Malignant Hypertension

Though rare, malignant hypertension is the most ominous form of high blood pressure. It's marked by an unusually sudden rise in blood pressure to dangerous levels, often with the diastolic reading reaching 120–130 mm/Hg or higher. However, it may also occur at lower, seemingly more normal blood pressure levels if the rise is particularly abrupt. Unlike other kinds of hypertension, it's usually accompanied by dramatic symptoms such as severe headache, shortness of breath, chest pain, nausea and vomiting, blurred vision or even blindness, seizures, and loss of consciousness.

Malignant hypertension is a medical emergency. It places people at immediate risk for heart attack, stroke, heart failure, permanent kidney damage, and bleeding in the brain. Anyone who develops the condition must be hospitalized immediately. Malignant hypertension develops in less than 1 percent of people who already have high blood pressure. In rare cases, the appearance of malignant hypertension is the first sign that a person has high blood pressure. While the cause of this condition is unknown, you should never stop taking your antihypertensive medication without your doctor's supervision. Doing so might cause a precipitous increase in your blood pressure and put you at risk.

So You've Been Diagnosed with Hypertension

Once a diagnosis of hypertension is confirmed, the next step is to determine whether target-organ damage (atherosclerosis, heart disease, stroke, or kidney disease) has occurred and to determine whether yours is primary or secondary hypertension.

Expect to undergo a thorough evaluation, including a medical history, physical examination, laboratory tests, and possibly other diagnostic exams such as a chest x-ray. When a health care professional takes your history, mention any recent changes in weight, physical activity, alcohol consumption, or tobacco use. Also, list all the prescription and over-the-counter medications, herbal products, and even any illegal drugs you're taking or have recently taken. Some of the substances found in these products can raise blood pressure or interfere with blood pressure medication.

Other medical tests can also be helpful. Routine urine and blood analyses can reveal medical conditions. For instance, protein or blood in the urine may be a sign of kidney damage, while increased glucose suggests diabetes. Blood tests typically measure sodium, potassium, chloride, calcium, bicarbonate, glucose, and cholesterol, as well as urea nitrogen or creatinine, which are indicators of kidney function. If your doctor suspects that you have another condition or target-organ damage, he or she may order further tests.

An electrocardiogram (EKG or ECG), which measures electrical activity of the heart and gives a general picture of the heart's health, is especially important. The initial EKG is called a *baseline*. Subsequent EKGs can be compared with the original to reveal changes that may indicate heart disease or left ventricular hypertrophy (LVH).

An exercise stress test assesses how your cardiovascular system responds to physical activity. The test monitors the electrical activity of your heart and your blood pressure during exercise, which usually involves pedaling a stationary bike or walking on a treadmill. A stress test can reveal problems that aren't apparent when you're at rest. If you have high blood pressure, the information from this test must be considered before you start an exercise program.

Chest pain, dizzy spells, palpitations, or other symptoms may indicate heart disease, which calls for additional testing. For instance, your physician may order Holter monitoring, in which you wear a portable device that takes a continuous EKG recording for twenty-four hours or longer. Another test is the echocardiogram, which uses ultrasound waves to show your heart in motion. It's used to diagnose thickening of the heart wall, valve defects, blood clots, and excessive fluid around the heart.

Symptoms such as urinary tract infections, frequent urination, or pain in your flank (low down on the side of your abdomen) may be signs of a kidney disorder. If the doctor hears a bruit—the sound of a rush of blood—through a stethoscope placed on the flank, it may be a sign of renal artery stenosis, discussed earlier. You may have to undergo blood analyses and imaging tests to learn whether a kidney problem is causing your hypertension.

When Is Medication Necessary?

If you've been diagnosed with any level of hypertension—even prehypertension—you may wonder if you're effectively sentenced to a lifetime of daily medication. The JNC 7 recommends incorporating lifestyle modifications (which we will discuss later in this book) if you are diagnosed with prehypertension. It also recommends starting drug therapy in people with average blood pressure readings greater than 140/90 mm/Hg. The goal of therapy is to achieve a blood pressure below 140/90 mm/Hg, or below 130/80 mm/Hg in people with diabetes or kidney disease. We will explore the many available drug treatments for hypertension in Chapter 6.

Why Is Hypertension Dangerous?

Hypertension makes your heart work harder to do its job. Isn't that a good thing? After all, a little hard work never hurt anyone, right? Well, in the case of human hearts, it most certainly does. The intense pounding of blood gradually damages the arterial walls. Small arteries are especially vulnerable. The walls respond by thickening and losing their elasticity and strength. As a result, less blood can pass through them, depriving surrounding tissues of oxygen and nutrients. The vessel walls are also more prone to rupture. Eventually, hypertension damages not just the blood vessels themselves, but the target organs of the disease: the heart, brain, kidneys, and eyes. The longer you have hypertension, the greater your chances of developing target-organ damage and, consequently, serious conditions such as heart disease, stroke, kidney disease, and eye damage.

When vessel walls are damaged, they become inflamed. This inflammation and consequent thickening in turn encourages a buildup of debris called *plaque* made up of fats, or cholesterol. When this arterial plaque builds up, as shown in Figure 1.3, the vessels narrow and atherosclerosis develops, which further restricts blood flow and thus makes the heart work even harder.

By making your blood vessel walls more susceptible to atherosclerosis, hypertension increases your risk of having a stroke or a heart attack. When coronary arteries become narrowed by plaque

FIGURE 1.3 Atherosclerosis

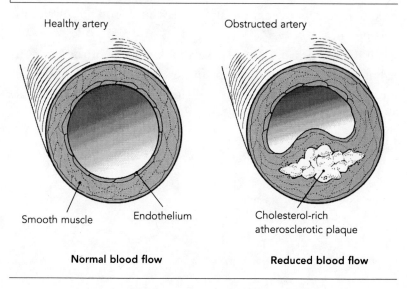

Healthy artery   Obstructed artery

Smooth muscle   Endothelium   Cholesterol-rich atherosclerotic plaque

Normal blood flow   **Reduced blood flow**

and a blood clot (thrombus) forms over the narrowed artery, a heart attack results. Fragments from these deposits—called *emboli*—can also break away, travel through the bloodstream, and eventually block other vessels, such as those supplying the legs (causing circulatory problems) or the brain (causing a stroke).

Your heart will automatically beat harder when you are jogging or when you are suddenly cut off in traffic while driving. This increase is normal as the sympathetic nervous system kicks in, so that oxygen-rich blood can get to your organs and you have the energy to deal with the situation. That's not hypertension. Once you stop jogging or get out of harm's way, your blood pressure should return to normal. With hypertension, your blood pressure remains elevated after the challenge has gone away.

Next Steps

Now that you understand why it's so important to keep your blood pressure in the "safe" zone, it's time to get down to business. The remainder of this book is about giving you the tools you need to create lasting change and to get your blood pressure numbers down.

In the next chapter, we'll take a look at some of the key contributors to hypertension, explain how to take your blood pressure, and begin to discuss some of the ways you can make simple changes to lower your numbers.

CHAPTER 2

Understanding Why Hypertension Develops

As we mentioned in Chapter 1, the vast majority of people with hypertension have primary, or essential, hypertension, which means that instead of being linked to some other underlying health condition, it is likely the result of some combination of risk factors. A risk factor is, as the name implies, anything that can increase your chances of developing hypertension. If you've already been diagnosed with hypertension, it might sound a bit redundant to talk about the risk factors for developing it. Not so fast. Knowing what likely contributed to your condition is the first step toward managing it; taking responsibility for those risk factors is the second.

In this chapter we will explore the major risk factors for hypertension and then present two case studies of patients who participated in our Cardiac Wellness Program at the Mind/Body Medical Institute (M/BMI). In subsequent chapters we'll go into diet, exercise, and stress management in greater detail, and also help you to create the personalized program that is just right for you.

Risk factors can be divided into two major categories: those you cannot change, and those you can.

Risk Factors You Cannot Change

Even though you cannot control certain risk factors, that doesn't mean that you should forget about them. In fact, being aware of them can help you put your overall cardiovascular risk profile into perspective and may provide you with extra incentive to be especially vigilant in addressing those risk factors that you can change.

- **Genetics.** Hypertension, like many health conditions, runs in families. If one (or both) of your parents or a sibling suffers from hypertension, your odds of developing it are increased. Research indicates that about 25 percent of cases of essential hypertension in families have a genetic basis. This doesn't mean, however, that it's a sure thing. Indeed, some of the similarities observed in families may be the result of environmental influences. Children's eating patterns, coping skills, and propensity toward healthy and unhealthy habits are often shaped by their parents' behavior and the social climate in which they're raised.
- **Age.** Although aging doesn't invariably lead to hypertension, high blood pressure is more common in later years. Between ages thirty and sixty-five, systolic pressure increases an average of 20 mm/Hg, and it continues to climb after age seventy. This age-associated increase largely explains isolated systolic hypertension and is attributed to an increase in peripheral vascular resistance in the arteries.
- **Gender.** Men often show signs of hypertension in their late thirties, while women often develop hypertension after menopause. Women's blood pressures, especially the systolic readings, rise more sharply with age. Indeed, after age fifty-five, women are at greater risk for hypertension. This pattern may be explained in part by hormonal differences between the sexes. As the production of estrogen drops with menopause, women lose its beneficial effects and their blood pressure climbs.

- **Race.** African Americans show higher rates of hypertension than the rest of the population, and it tends to develop earlier and more aggressively. They are nearly twice as likely to suffer a fatal stroke, one and a half times more likely to die from heart disease, and four times more likely to suffer kidney failure than are Caucasians. Hypertension is the number-one cause of death in African Americans.

Risk Factors You *Can* Change

The following risk factors are the basis for the lifestyle modification program described in this book. They represent opportunities for making dramatic improvements, even from seemingly small changes. In later chapters we'll discuss how improving on these risk factors can lower your blood pressure. But first, let's look at how they contribute to hypertension.

- **Smoking.** Doctors have long known that smoking promotes heart disease, but for a long time smoking didn't appear to have a direct connection to hypertension. More recent investigations have revealed a crucial link that earlier studies missed, because blood pressure is generally measured in doctors' offices and clinics where smoking is prohibited.

   When researchers tested blood pressure while people smoked, they discovered that within five minutes of lighting up, the subjects' systolic pressures rose dramatically—more than 20 mm/Hg on average—before gradually declining to their original levels over the following thirty minutes. This means the typical smoker's blood pressure soars many times throughout the day. Like people with labile hypertension (in which blood pressure may jump frequently in response to daily stresses), smokers may suffer "part-time" hypertension. For example, smokers with a prehypertensive reading of less than 140/90 mm/Hg may actually reach stage 1 hypertension every time they puff a cigarette.

This increase occurs because nicotine, whether smoked or chewed, constricts blood vessels, forcing the heart to work harder. As a result, the heart rate and blood pressure increase. The chemicals in tobacco smoke raise heart disease risk in other ways, too. They can reduce the body's oxygen supply; lower levels of high-density lipoprotein (HDL), or "good" cholesterol; and make blood platelets more likely to stick together and form clots that can trigger a heart attack or stroke.

- **Obesity.** Excess weight and hypertension often go hand in hand, because carrying even a few extra pounds forces your heart to work harder. Obesity is defined as being more than 20 percent over your ideal body weight (IBW). According to the Framingham Heart Study, obese women have greater than eight times the chance of developing hypertension, as compared to women at their IBW. It's not weight alone that matters, but also where you carry your extra weight. People with excess fat above the hips—the so-called apple shape shown in Figure 2.1—are at greater risk for hypertension, high cholesterol, and diabetes.

FIGURE 2.1 Distribution of Body Weight

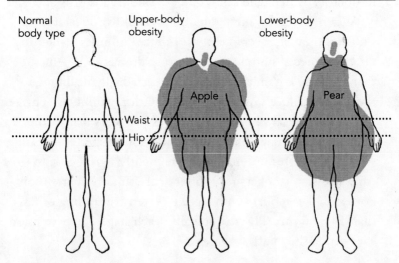

- **Sedentary lifestyle.** Compared with the physically active, couch potatoes are significantly more likely to develop hypertension and suffer heart attacks. Like any muscle, your heart gets stronger with exercise. A stronger heart pumps blood more efficiently. Other cardiovascular benefits of exercise include losing excess weight, increasing HDL levels, and decreasing triglycerides (fat from foods that becomes part of the blood circulating in the bloodstream).
- **Excess salt.** Federal guidelines advise limiting sodium intake to less than 2,300 milligrams (mg) per day for all Americans (about the amount in one teaspoon of table salt) and less than 1,500 mg for people with hypertension, older adults, and African Americans. Yet Americans typically consume 3,300 to 6,000 mg a day. Nearly 50 percent of people who have hypertension are salt sensitive, meaning eating too much sodium clearly elevates their blood pressure. In addition, diabetics, the obese, and the elderly seem more sensitive to the effects of salt than the general population.
- **Caffeine.** Most studies provide no clear indication that moderate caffeine intake (less than 100 mg a day) causes hypertension.
- **Alcohol use.** Many studies have linked excess alcohol intake to hypertension. Excessive drinking, defined as having three or more drinks per day, is a factor in about 7 percent of hypertension cases. Women with hypertension should have no more than one drink per day, and men should have no more than two.
- **Stress.** Stress clearly plays a role in hypertension. As your stress level decreases, so does your blood pressure.

Measuring Your Blood Pressure at Home

Measuring your blood pressure at home can be a valuable complement to having it checked in your doctor's office, but it is not a substitute. Checking your blood pressure at home is quick and painless. Stress, excessive exercise, and even a few drinks the night before your doctor's appointment can push your blood pressure up. So it is often difficult to tell whether an unusually high reading in the office really reflects your usual blood pressure readings during the week.

Therefore, people with hypertension are often encouraged to monitor blood pressure on their own. Home monitoring is especially useful for people with white-coat hypertension and labile hypertension, as well as to track responses to exercise, medications, or changes in treatment.

Home Blood Pressure Kits

Manual blood pressure kits, some of which include a stethoscope, are similar to those used by health care professionals. Manual blood pressure models are the least expensive but are difficult to master. You must wrap the cuff around your arm, pump it up, and listen through the stethoscope while simultaneously turning a valve to deflate the cuff and watching the needle gauge. People with average manual dexterity, eyesight, and hearing often master this procedure easily, but if you are hampered by arthritis, vision problems, or hearing loss, you may need someone to assist you. Or you may be better off with an electronic monitor.

Electronic monitors, which measure your blood pressure without the use of a stethoscope and display your blood pressure readings digitally, are easy to handle alone and are relatively inexpensive. You can choose from a manual arm cuff (which you inflate yourself by squeezing a rubber bulb), an automatic arm cuff (which you inflate by touching a button), or an automatic wrist cuff model. Those with arm cuffs have received the highest ratings for accuracy. Electronic monitors have various features, such as memory recall of the last blood pressure measurement or fuzzy logic that will automatically pump the cuff up only as much as is necessary for each reading.

Ambulatory Blood Pressure

Occasionally, your doctor may send you home with a device that automatically takes your blood pressure every fifteen to thirty minutes over the course of a twenty-four-hour period and records the results. After reviewing the data, your doctor should have a better sense of your usual blood pressure. You would receive verbal and written instructions for the monitoring procedure and a diary to record the time you sleep and take medication, as well as posture, activity, and any symptoms related to your condition. The arm needs to be kept immobile at the time of measurement. Current monitors are generally lightweight, easy to wear on the arm, accurate, and quiet.

Blood Pressure Position

The last time a health care professional checked your blood pressure, were you sitting, standing, or lying down? Was your arm flexed at the elbow or hanging at your side? The answers to these questions matter; the position of your body and arm can change a blood pressure reading by 10 percent or more. That could be enough to change the classification of your blood pressure, start you on a drug you don't really need, or lead your doctor to adjust your medications incorrectly.

National and international guidelines offer specific instructions for measuring blood pressure. They say you should sit quietly for five minutes with your feet on the floor and have your arm flexed at heart level during the measurement.

Researchers at the University of California–San Diego wanted to see just how much blood pressure was affected by body and arm positions. They asked one hundred volunteers to have their pressure measured six times: while sitting, standing, and lying down, once with the arm at a ninety-degree angle to the chest and once with it parallel to the body in each position. Standing with the arm hanging at the side yielded the highest blood pressure readings, whereas lying down with the arm flexed yielded the lowest.

The Right Way

Which measurement gives your true blood pressure? That's hard to say. Blood pressure changes constantly. In addition to following a daily cycle (often highest in the morning and lowest in the evening), it responds to what you are doing, thinking, and feeling. So the reading from your doctor's office is just a snapshot that may or may not reflect your usual condition.

The seated-with-arm-flexed measurement is in keeping with current blood pressure guidelines, the same ones doctors use to decide when and how to treat high blood pressure. That doesn't necessarily make it better. But it does make the case for consistency. Following the same procedure every time removes body or arm position as a possible factor in blood pressure variation. That way you can tell if your blood pressure has truly changed or has remained stable.

Going Through the Motions

Whether you are taking your blood pressure at home or having it measured by your doctor, following these steps will get rid of variables that can throw off the reading. If a health care professional isn't doing it right, don't hesitate to ask him or her to follow the guidelines.

- Don't drink a caffeinated beverage or smoke during the thirty minutes before the test.
- Sit quietly for five minutes.
- During the measurement, sit in a chair with your feet on the floor and your arm supported so your elbow is at about heart level.
- The inflatable part of the cuff should encircle at least 80 percent of your arm, and the cuff should be placed on bare skin, not over a shirt.
- Don't talk during the measurement.

There are times to break these rules. If you sometimes feel light-headed when getting out of bed in the morning or when

you stand after sitting, you should have your blood pressure checked while seated and then while standing to see if it falls from one position to the next.

It is important to keep a record of your blood pressure readings at home so that you can review them with your doctor.

Carol's Story

Carol, a former counselor, is a forty-six-year-old, married, stay-at-home mom with a six-year-old child. She has a history of hypertension and elevated cholesterol, which she has managed for eight years with the drugs Zestril and Lipitor. She is a former smoker and also has a significant family history with a sibling who suffered a heart attack at age thirty-nine.

When we first met Carol, she described significant stress in her life. She reported feeling irritable frequently, which was affecting her relationship with her husband. She also felt she often overreacted to minor issues with her son. Her initial evaluation indicated that she scored high on symptoms of depression and anxiety. In addition, she scored low on her ability to manage stress. Her stress warning signs included almost daily bruxism (grinding the teeth) and headaches. We knew that in order to help Carol, teaching her stress management skills was going to be a priority.

Carol knew she had to trust the recommendations that we gave her. She welcomed learning new ways to manage stress. She began eliciting the relaxation response on a daily basis (we will discuss these and other stress management techniques in Chapter 3). Carol learned how to identify her negative thinking patterns in a situation and to restructure these thoughts in a more positive and meaningful way.

During our thirteen-week program, Carol learned—just as you will—to combine stress management with nutrition and exercise for a total lifestyle program. She began walking more (which she admits was challenging at first) and began to incorporate more sensible food choices into her and her family's diet. All the while, she remained dedicated to her newfound stress management skills.

At the end of her thirteen weeks, Carol had made significant progress. She reported feeling more calm and focused. She learned not to overextend herself and also reported feeling much healthier physically and emotionally. She had learned not to sweat the small things in her life and to listen more and be less judgmental. She and her husband had decided to adopt a baby over the next six months, and they were eager to help a child who was not as fortunate as they were.

Then there were those all-important blood pressure numbers. Carol had successfully lowered her readings from an average 146/86 mm/Hg to 125/80 mm/Hg within thirteen weeks. Her cholesterol dropped too—by 50 points. Her test scores reflected a significant decrease in symptoms of depression and anxiety. She had truly learned to embrace a healthier lifestyle.

John's Story

John is a forty-eight-year-old married CEO of an environmental company. He had been diagnosed with hypertension at age eighteen. John didn't tolerate blood pressure drugs well but was taking Norvasc when he came to see us. He had a family history of hypertension, with both his parents and his sister also having the disease. "I kept asking my doctor, 'Isn't there another way to lower my blood pressure without medication?'" he says. "Finally he told me about the M/BMI."

John was a self-confessed "sweet-tooth guy," and it showed. At 221 pounds, John was obese, with a body mass index of 34. We knew that to get John's blood pressure lower, he would have to take off a good deal of that weight through nutrition management and physical activity. (He was interested in learning to elicit the relaxation response, which he did, but his test scores indicated that stress was not a significant problem.)

John enjoyed physical activity, but finding time in his busy life for regular exercise was a challenge. Also, he seemed to be an advocate of the old adage "no pain, no gain," believing that for exercise to have value, it had to be intense and vigorous. Helping John not only to make time in his life for regular exercise but also to adopt a more flexible approach became our focus. When he did have time, he enjoyed basketball, using his stationary bike, and walking. He joined a gym near his workplace and began exercising at lunchtime. Following our recommendations, he began to balance his workouts between aerobics, flexibility, and resistance training. He varied his routine based on how he felt each day, always keeping in mind his goals of doing aerobic exercise four to five times per week and resistance training two to three times per week. He surprised himself by finding that if he couldn't fit his exercise in at lunch, he would carve out time to ride the stationary bike at home before dinner.

John's diet required major changes, and it was tough to know where to begin. He needed to decide what he felt ready to change about his diet and what would make a significant difference to his health. One specific issue was that he ate "comfort food" when under stress, especially ice cream—sometimes a bowl a day. His diet was also high in refined starches such as white bread and pasta, as well as sugar and fat.

During his thirteen weeks with us, John was able to cut back significantly on his beloved ice cream, and he also started to substitute whole grains, fruits, and vegetables for many of the refined, sugary, salty, and fatty foods he had eaten before. (Carefully reading food labels for fat and sodium content quickly became a habit.) What turned out to be one of the most important changes he made was to take lunch from home every day rather than buying whatever the cafeteria had to offer.

By the end of the program, John had decreased his blood pressure from an average of 161/81 mm/Hg to an average of 140/76 mm/Hg with half the dose of blood pressure medicine. He lost ten pounds, two and a half inches from his waist, and one and a half inches from his hips.

Next Steps

Carol's and John's stories are impressive but not uncommon. We've seen people from all walks of life surprise themselves by the remarkable changes they've been able to make. Some of them still can't believe it themselves, but we can. That's because we know these techniques work. We've proven it time and again. How will your story read? What lifestyle changes will you make? Only time and your dedication to this program will tell.

Let's get started right now. Let's begin the journey that can help you lower your blood pressure in the same way that Carol and John did. In the next chapter, we'll get started with the relaxation response, which is the foundation of all our teachings at M/BMI.

3

Managing Stress

No doubt, stress is something you're well familiar with. Who isn't? Traffic jams, deadlines, bills, money worries, the workplace, family demands, relationships, and health—these are but a few of the day-to-day stressors we encounter.

The problem is that most of us don't know how to manage our stress. Glance at the ten leading causes of death in America, and you won't find the word *stress* anywhere. Yet many well-respected studies link stress to heart disease and stroke—two of the top ten killers. Heart disease alone is responsible for nearly one in three deaths. Chronic stress may contribute to or exacerbate many health problems, including hypertension.

In this chapter, we'll be taking a user's tour through the stress mechanisms of the mind and body and looking at some of the practical steps you can take to better manage stress.

Using Version-1 Software in the Modern World

Eliciting the stress response to a physical danger is something our ancestors knew well. Back when they still lived in caves, there was little to think about apart from daily survival. Any day with enough food and shelter to continue living was a good day. It wasn't always easy. Lions and tigers and bears (oh, my!) were also prowling around with their own survival to think about.

Physical Health Problems Affected by Stress

- Allergic skin reactions
- Chronic constipation
- Chronic pain
- Diabetes
- Dizziness
- Heart problems, such as angina and cardiac arrhythmias
- Heartburn
- Hypertension
- Infertility
- Irritable bowel syndrome
- Menopausal symptoms, such as hot flashes
- Persistent fatigue
- Premenstrual syndrome
- Insomnia

So in order to give prehistoric humans a fighting chance, nature developed a bit of "software" to help them either confront threatening situations head-on or to escape altogether—an involuntary response to help them deal with danger and live to see another day. You've probably heard of it before: the fight-or-flight response, also known as the *stress response*.

The world has, of course, changed a lot since the days of our cave-dwelling kin, but the human body has not. In other words, many of us still use the same antiquated coping mechanisms when dealing with day-to-day stressors that our ancient ancestors used when confronted by a physical danger.

Introduction to the Stress Response

The stress response is an innate physiological response designed to prepare your mind and body to deal with a physical threat. For your ancestors, a threatening situation meant staring down a saber-toothed tiger; for you, it means juggling work and home life or worrying about the bills. Your mind and body automatically shift into gear, eliciting the stress response. The problem is that your mind does a poor job of differentiating between a real physical danger and a day-to-day hassle.

When you encounter something stressful, real or imagined, the cerebral cortex, the part of your brain that controls consciousness, sends out a three-pronged alert to your body. Each of the three pathways involved in the stress response—illustrated in Figure 3.1—activates a particular set of resources that are essential to survival in times of real, physical danger.

One pathway involves the musculoskeletal system. A part of the brain known as the *motor cortex* sends signals directly to the muscles, increasing muscle tension. As a result, the muscles in your jaw, shoulders, and back tighten. You are physically braced to encounter a threat or to run away.

The second pathway is initiated when your cerebral cortex stimulates the hypothalamus, a part of the brain that regulates the two major components of the nervous system: the sympathetic nervous system, which revs up the body in response to perceived dangers, and the parasympathetic nervous system, which calms the body after the danger has passed. The hypothalamus simultaneously mobilizes certain parts of the body to respond to a perceived threat while conserving the body's energy elsewhere. For example, the sound of screeching car tires behind you stimulates the sympathetic nervous system to release the hormones adrenaline and noradrenaline. Heart rate, blood pressure, and the volume of blood being pumped out of the heart all increase. Your blood platelets become stickier to help clot your blood. At the same time, the parasympathetic nervous system slows down activity in other parts of the body that are not needed in an emergency. Less blood reaches areas such as the skin and stomach, your hands and feet get cold, and the repair and growth of body tissues and bones slow down.

The third pathway is activated when the hypothalamus stimulates the pituitary gland. Cells in the pituitary then send their own chemical messenger to the adrenal glands, which release cor-

FIGURE 3.1 HPA Axis and the Stress Response

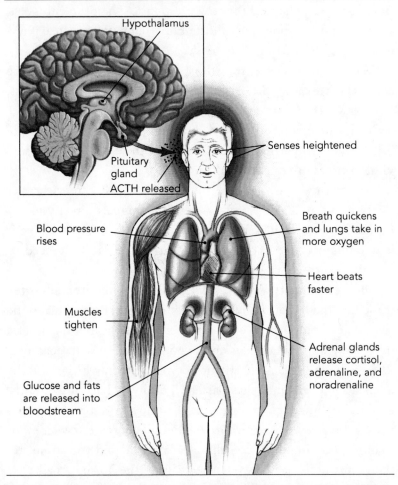

Hypothalamus

Pituitary gland

ACTH released

Senses heightened

Blood pressure rises

Breath quickens and lungs take in more oxygen

Heart beats faster

Muscles tighten

Adrenal glands release cortisol, adrenaline, and noradrenaline

Glucose and fats are released into bloodstream

The hypothalamus, pituitary gland, and adrenal glands make up the HPA axis, which plays a pivotal role in triggering the stress response. By releasing certain chemicals, such as adrenocorticotropic hormone (ACTH) and cortisol, the HPA axis rouses the body for action when it's faced with a stressor. As the illustration reveals, the effect of this release of hormones is widespread. Senses become sharper, muscles tighten, the heart beats faster, blood pressure rises, and breathing quickens. All of this prepares you to fight or flee in the face of danger.

tisol and aldosterone into the bloodstream. Surges of these hormones boost immune function into overdrive. If this hormonal rush is sustained, however, the immune system begins to wear out, compromising the body's internal defenses.

What's Stressful?

Which of the following events do you suppose most people would find stressful: losing a job, winning the lottery, buying a home, being promoted at work, going on vacation, or making a major personal accomplishment? If you guessed all of them, then you're absolutely right. What we now know is that feelings of stress are rooted in response to change. Whether it's that split-second change in perceived physical safety or the more subtle change that comes with being stuck in traffic, stress can be defined as the physical, mental, and emotional reaction over the short and long term to changes in one's environment.

Several decades ago, two psychiatrists at the University of Washington devised a scale for researchers that weighed the stress of major life events. While many of the items on the forty-three-item list don't apply to many of us, here are the top ten, as they relate to a 100-point scale:

1. Death of spouse or partner: 100
2. Divorce: 73
3. Marriage or partnership separation: 65
4. Jail term: 63
5. Death of a close family member: 63
6. Injury or illness: 53
7. Marriage: 50
8. Fired from job: 47
9. Marriage reconciliation: 45
10. Retirement: 45

Is Stress a Problem for You?

At this point, you might be saying, "Wait! The jitters I get before a meeting with my boss are nowhere near as intense as the heart-pounding terror of a physical threat." That's true. What's more, different people often react differently to the very same situation. We might call this difference a matter of one's stress tolerance or hardiness. Some people are naturally hardier than others; some have to work on becoming hardier. But the bottom line remains: those who do not take steps to control their stress are fated to be controlled by it.

In the course of a lifetime, odds are good that you'll survive some very stressful events. You'll also face a gamut of far smaller day-to-day stressors. But as we mentioned before, too much stress can affect your physical and emotional health. Trouble usually brews when the stress response is repeatedly evoked, causing unnecessary wear and tear on the body. According to one estimate, the fight-or-flight switch can flick on and off in Americans as many as fifty times a day. In a world bursting with situations that can elicit the stress response, many health experts believe this is cause for concern.

Stress becomes a problem when it is more than a normal part of life and a chronic part of daily life. It's when stress becomes an underlying part of how you feel and think that its residual effects begin to seep into seemingly unrelated facets of your life and may even begin to damage your health. So let's see if stress is a problem for you.

The Many Faces of Chronic Stress

The lists in this section will help you recognize some common stress warning signs. Once you're aware of how stress makes you feel and act, you can use the tools described in the following pages to help you manage it better.

Warning Signs

Stress makes itself known in many forms, but none as immediate and powerful as its physical symptoms. The following are some of the most common:

- Stiff or tense muscles
- Backaches
- Headaches

- Sleep problems
- Tiredness
- Fast heartbeat
- Shakiness or tremors
- Sweating
- Ringing in the ears
- Dizziness or fainting
- Grinding the teeth
- Stomachache, nausea
- Restlessness
- Loss of interest in sex

Just as many physical symptoms can strike at any time, so too can any of the following emotional, behavioral, and cognitive warning signs:

- Anxiety
- Depression
- Anger
- Quick temper
- Overly critical attitude
- Crying
- Sense of loneliness
- Loss of sense of humor
- Indecisiveness
- Lack of creativity
- Poor concentration
- Trouble thinking
- Feeling of a lack of meaning in life and pursuits

Automatic Thoughts

Stress has a way of turning your mind into a runaway train. Negative thoughts follow other negative thoughts until you're fully consumed by worry, anxiety, anger, or doubt. You may start with a simple thought, such as "The bus is late," only to have it drift out of control: "I'll be late for work. I won't make it to my meeting on time. My boss will be angry with me. My job is in jeopardy." Sometimes even seemingly happy thoughts hurtle down the wrong track. "Wonderful, the lab report says my biopsy results are negative!" can quickly turn into "I wonder how good that lab is? Maybe the results were positive, and the lab didn't pick it up. Cancer that's undetected gets worse. By the time the error is found, it could be too late."

These scenarios are examples of automatic thoughts. They can engage the stress response almost as easily as a growling Doberman can by bounding in your direction.

So too can the barrage of negative thoughts that many people play through their minds on an endless loop or flip on automatically when faced with certain people or situations. Thoughts that include the words *must*, *should*, *always*, and *never* often reflect rigid thinking that could stand to be softened. Familiar examples of automatic thoughts might include, "Oh, no. Why me? I'll never get this done, nothing will ever change, and this always happens to me." The voice may be yours or that of someone else in your life, such as an overly critical parent. Even in the absence of obviously stressful situations, this inner critic can make you miserable and stressed.

Cognitive Distortions

Automatic thoughts often contain cognitive distortions. Some common cognitive distortions appear in the following list. They are based on theories of cognitive therapy developed by Aaron T. Beck, M.D., which were further refined and brought to popular attention by David D. Burns, M.D. Do any of these distortions resonate with you? Use this list to make yourself aware of the games your mind plays.

- **All or nothing.** If you don't perform flawlessly, you consider yourself a complete failure.
- **Overgeneralization.** One negative event, such as a slight from your spouse or an encounter with a dishonest merchant, fits into an endless pattern of dismaying

circumstances and defeat. For example, you might think you're unattractive or that you can't trust anyone.

- **Mental filter.** One negative episode, such as a rude comment made to you during an otherwise enjoyable evening, shades everything else like a drop of food coloring in a glass of water.
- **Jumping to conclusions.** You draw negative conclusions without checking to see whether they have any foundation in fact. You may be mind reading: "My friend seems upset. She must be mad at me." Or you may be fortune telling: "I just know the results of my medical test won't be good."
- **Magnification or minimization.** You exaggerate potential problems or mistakes until they snowball into a catastrophe. Or you minimize anything that might make you feel good, such as appreciation for a kind act you did or the recognition that other people have flaws too.
- **"Should" statements.** You adhere to a rigid set of beliefs and internal rules about what you should be doing. For example, if you're held up by a traffic accident on the freeway, you think, "I should have left earlier."
- **Labeling.** Rather than describe a mistake or challenge in your life, you label yourself negatively (a screwup). When another person's behavior bothers you, you pin a global label on him or her (controlling, a jerk).

The remainder of this chapter will focus on two powerful tools for combating stress and negative thinking: the relaxation response and cognitive restructuring.

The Relaxation Response: Short-Circuiting Stress

As we mentioned before, the stress response is the result of the same survival software the human body has been running on since ancient times. You can't uninstall it, but you can upgrade it with some knowledge and practice. In fact, you must do so for the sake of your health and quality of life. When you're feeling stressed out, you're in a reactive mode. Your emotions have taken the driver's seat, and you're focused very intently on the problem rather than possible solutions. But understand this: when you're in that reactive mode, in order to regain control, you're going to have to stage something of an emotional coup d'état. Where do you start? Well, it's not by attempting to remove stressors from your life. That's just not possible. Rather, you're going to start by learning about your mind and body's natural antidote to the stress response: the relaxation response.

Just as the stress response is a state of heightened alertness and physical preparedness, the relaxation response leads to a quieting of the sympathetic nervous system. Oxygen consumption within the body drops steeply. Your heartbeat and breathing slow down. Research shows that regularly invoking the relaxation response leads to lasting declines in high blood pressure.

How does it work? Remember that in the stress response, your sympathetic nervous system sets off an explosion of involuntary responses throughout the body: the heart rate and breath quicken, muscles tense, thoughts race. The relaxation response is a physiological shift that puts the brakes on the runaway biological changes that put you into overdrive. It is the opposite state to the stress response; however, unlike the stress response, the relaxation response is a learned reaction. If you're ready, let's learn to elicit that response.

Learning the Relaxation Response

Thinking about the relaxation response might conjure up an image of the serene Zen monk lost in meditation somewhere high in the Himalayas. While it's true that attaining deep states of meditation is an integral part of many of the world's spiritual practices and faith traditions, learning the relaxation response doesn't require years of austere devotion. All it requires is a bit of practice and a willingness to set aside some time each day. There are many different ways to elicit it. You can find one that suits you best or mix it up by putting several techniques into your regimen.

The major techniques we'll cover to elicit the relaxation response are:

- Diaphragmatic breathing
- Meditation
- Progressive muscle relaxation
- Guided imagery

Let's take a look at each.

Diaphragmatic Breathing. Take a deep breath. Go ahead, take one. Breath is a funny thing. Most of the time it's controlled involuntarily by your body, so that you can focus your attention on other things. At other times you can let your mind control it, insofar as you have the ability to consciously regulate the depth and rhythm of your breathing. For this reason, many people throughout history have considered the breath something of a bridge between the mind and the body, which is why it plays such a prominent role in mind-body practices such as yoga and meditation.

As we've already discussed, one of the components of the stress response is shallow, rapid breathing. By consciously reversing the pattern of upper-chest breathing to diaphragmatic breathing, we can essentially hack into the software that's causing us to feel excessive stress.

Learning to breathe from the diaphragm is really quite easy:

1. Find a comfortable, quiet place to sit or lie down.
2. Place one hand on your chest and the other on your abdomen, just below your belly button. Take a slow, deep breath. Your lower hand should move more than the hand on your chest.
3. Concentrate on letting your abdomen expand fully, drawing air down into your lungs. Notice your belly rising and falling with each breath.
4. Now practice this breathing for several minutes.

Meditation. Meditation can be broadly defined as any activity that keeps your attention anchored in the present moment. The intention is to direct your concentration to a single focus—one sound, word, or image, or your breath. There are two basic approaches to meditation: concentrative meditation and mindfulness meditation. Concentrative meditation focuses the attention on the breath, an image, or a mantra in order to quiet the mind. Mindfulness meditation involves opening your attention to become aware of sensations and feelings without becoming involved in thinking about them. You simply witness whatever occurs. Meditation can take several different forms:

- **Repetitive prayer.** Several large studies have suggested a positive link between a strong religious or spiritual life and long-lasting health and happiness. Other studies have noted less hostility and anxiety, lower blood pressure, and a better quality of life among people with strong beliefs. Whatever the case, it's clear that prayer offers solace and comfort to many people.

  If prayer is meaningful to you, it can enhance the relaxation response and perhaps your health as well. You may want to use a short repetitive prayer or a religious phrase to help you focus.

- **Focus words.** Focus words or phrases can enhance your sense of peace, calm, and connection while you elicit the relaxation response. They may be secular or religious. They can have deep personal meaning or simply be pleasing sounds, but they should not be emotionally charged. Mentally, you might say one word or phrase as you breathe in and another as you breathe out, or just use one word or phrase on the exhalation. Some common examples are *peace*, *one*, *calm*, and *om*.

- **Mindfulness meditation.** Mindfulness meditation is an ancient Buddhist practice that induces the relaxation response. Today's world is one of whirlwind multitasking, where we're often called on to juggle several things at once.

Sure, it's sometimes helpful to be able to do this, but multitasking encourages racing thoughts. It can launch you into the future or the past rather than keep you rooted in the present. In contrast, mindfulness teaches you to live in the present and to experience each moment of your life as it unfolds.

This last form of meditation can often be one of the most helpful in combating stress. The steps for practicing are simple:

1. Sit on a straight-backed chair or cross-legged on the floor. Focus on breathing from your diaphragm.
2. Begin to widen your focus from your breath. Become aware of any specific sounds or sensations in your body. Embrace and consider each without judgment.
3. If your mind starts to race, shift your awareness back to your breath. Then expand your focus again.

A less formal approach to mindfulness can also encourage you to stay in the present and truly participate in your life. You can choose any task or moment to practice it. Whether you are playing with a child, performing a repetitive task such as dancing, cooking, or cleaning, or watching a sunset, remembering these three points will help:

- Start with a breath focus and return to it periodically, staying aware of each inhalation and exhalation.
- Proceed with the task or situation at hand slowly and with full concentration.
- Engage all of your senses fully so that you experience every sensation.

Peeling and eating an orange offers an excellent example. For a few moments, just concentrate on your breath moving in and out of your nostrils. Look at the orange, turning it over in your hands. Run your fingertips over its bumpy texture and absorb its vibrant color and light citrus scent. Consider how you feel when you anticipate eating the orange. As you peel it, engage your senses fully. Note the slight spray as your fingers dig into and peel back the hardened skin and soft white pith. How does the orange smell and feel now? Are you salivating? When you put a slice of it in your mouth and bite through the thin membrane into its juicy center, what sensations do you feel?

Try not to hurry through one mouthful of orange to get to the next. Slow down and stay in the moment. Before you swallow each portion of the orange, be aware of the rising desire to do so. Then note how it feels when you swallow. Remain fully aware throughout the experience. Mindful eating can help you eat healthier and less.

Progressive Muscle Relaxation. Progressive muscle relaxation (PMR) teaches you to isolate specific sets of muscles, tense them briefly, and then relax them. You do this methodically from head to toe and feel the difference between tension and relaxation. The sense of release can be profound. This exercise is especially helpful if your mind is racing, making it hard to settle down. Follow these steps as you begin PMR:

1. While sitting in a comfortable chair or lying down, take a deep breath, allowing your stomach to rise as you inhale and fall as you exhale. Slowly breathe this way for two minutes before you start.

2. Concentrate on one muscle set at a time. Consciously tighten these muscles as you slowly count from one to five, and then release the tense muscles while you take a slow, deep breath and allow any tension to ebb away. Use this counting and breathing sequence as you tighten and then relax each of the following muscle sets. Take your time, working slowly through each muscle group:
   - Your forehead and scalp
   - The muscles around your eyes
   - Your jaw

- Your neck
- Your back
- Your shoulders
- Your upper arms
- Your forearms
- Your hands
- Your chest
- Your abdomen
- Your pelvis and buttocks
- Your thighs
- Your knees and calves
- Your feet
- Your toes

3. Mentally check your entire body from your head to your toes for any residual tension. If you notice any tight areas, tense those muscles while you count from one to five. Then release the muscles as you take slow, deep breaths. Continue breathing deeply and slowly for as long as you like.

   Ultimately, try to have your session last twenty minutes.

Guided Imagery. Guided imagery, or visualization that conjures soothing scenes, can be a powerful way of evoking the relaxation response. The images you choose—whether places or experiences—should enhance the sensation of inner calm. Lush descriptions of sandy beaches, bubbling streams, and fields of flowers are often verbalized by the teacher of a meditation class or recorded on a tape or CD to help you see the scene in your mind. The image must be relaxing for you in order to be effective, so make sure that any recorded program you use or the imagery you evoke on your own is pleasant. (A field of flowers may be wonderful for some, but not for those who have severe hay fever!)

Guided imagery allows for engaging all the senses, and in some ways, it is quite similar to mindfulness meditation, except that the point of your focus happens to be an image in your mind. For example, you might imagine yourself lying on your back in a field, watching the clouds go by on a calm summer day. Your imagery might involve noticing the smell of the fresh grass and nearby flowers, feeling your weight supported by the ground beneath you, feeling the warmth of the air across your skin, and watching a particular cloud change shape as it slowly makes its way across your field of vision. Our example here uses a hot-air balloon image. For other options, refer to Appendix A, which contains five additional visualization exercises.

Before you start an imagery session, find a quiet place to sit or lie down. Arrange yourself comfortably, and clear your mind as you take a couple of minutes to breathe fully and switch gears from focusing on the world around you to the world within.

Imagine you are standing at the edge of a beautiful meadow. Let all of your senses become aware of your surroundings. What time of year is it? What time of day? As you walk through the meadow, what do you see—flowers, birds, colors? What do you hear—birds, the wind? What do you smell—the earth, flowers? What do you feel—the sunshine, the breeze, the grass under your feet?

Notice that in the middle of the meadow is a beautiful hot-air balloon. Look at the beautiful colors. As you walk up to it, you realize that you can take a ride in it. As you step slowly into the basket, you notice that there are small sandbags on the floor. Each sandbag has writing on it. As you look closer, you see that each sandbag represents some burden, stress, or concern in your life. Slowly pick up each sandbag, notice what burden in your life it represents, and then toss it over the side. As you do so, notice how much lighter you feel. Sit down comfortably in the basket. As the balloon gets lighter, it gently lifts off of the ground. You begin to feel more calm and your mind begins to feel quiet. You can choose to float among the clouds or travel to a safe place that you create in your mind. Enjoy this quiet time for several minutes.

When you feel ready, slowly return to the meadow. Remember, this is a special hot-air balloon and you don't have to pick up your burdens to return to the ground. The balloon slowly and gently returns to the meadow on its own. Gently step out of the balloon and begin to walk back through the meadow, again paying attention to the scene around you. As you reach the edge of the meadow, slowly transition back to the room you're in. Open your eyes feeling refreshed and calm.

How to Develop Regular Practice

The first step for many people is finding the time in their daily lives. Don't worry, it's there. If you have time to be stressed, you have time to elicit the relaxation response. The most obvious times are in the early morning before beginning your day or in the late evening just before retiring. If your schedule is more flexible (as it may be for those who are retired, who stay at home with children, or who work part-time), then you may find it easier to take time during the middle of the day. Sticking consistently with a particular time of day will enable you to develop a routine.

The next step is to gradually increase the frequency and duration of your relaxation response. While daily practice is best, you may initially feel more comfortable practicing for fifteen minutes, three times a week. You may set a goal to add one day per week for a month, so that at the end of the month, you're practicing for fifteen minutes each day. This way the change will be gradual and not overwhelming. From there you may experiment with adding five minutes to every other session and eventually to every session, so that you're consistently practicing for fifteen to twenty minutes every day.

What if you don't stick to the schedule you've drawn up? It happens. Sometimes unexpected events come up. Sometimes people feel frustrated that they're not making enough progress quickly enough. Sometimes people just forget or don't feel like practicing on a particular day. Try not to feel discouraged. As we said, the relaxation response is a skill and a habit. If you slip up now and then, it doesn't mean that you've failed. Slips are normal and should be expected once in a while. Consider what got in the way and whether you set out to do too much. Ask yourself what strategies could help you overcome these barriers next week. Finally, embrace what felt good and find the opportunity to repeat it.

The third step is to learn to let go. When intrusive thoughts arise, as they inevitably will, simply notice their presence—with-

41

Carol's Story

If you've ever cared for young children, then you know a thing or two (or three) about stress. Carol is a forty-six-year-old stay-at-home mother of a six-year-old child. "I move at a pretty good clip all day," she says. Carol came to the Mind/Body Medical Institute when her doctor wanted to increase her current dose of hypertension medication. She had developed hypertension and high cholesterol about eight years before and will likely remain on medication for the remainder of her life. Wanting to take a more holistic approach rather than increase her medication dosage, Carol entered our Cardiac Wellness Program. "Meditation was going to be key in getting my blood pressure down," she says.

She began with small changes—a little bit here, a little bit there. "For a while, I'd do it, but I didn't feel like I was getting much benefit. But the more I did it, the easier it was to focus. I liked guided imagery the best." Now, after two months, she has successfully made a minimum of twenty minutes of daily meditation (along with improved diet and exercise) an integral part of her life. According to Carol, life seems a little bit easier. "I feel more relaxed. If I'm five minutes late, then I'm five minutes late. I have learned not to sweat the small things."

out judgment or expectation—and then let them pass by so that you can return your focus. In the beginning, you may find your mind wandering quite a bit. Don't let it frustrate you. With patience and practice, your relaxation sessions will become increasingly focused and rewarding.

Minirelaxation Response Exercises: Stress Relief on the Go

Minirelaxation response exercises can be practiced anywhere, often without anyone nearby being the wiser. Although they don't bestow the full, long-term benefits of exercises that induce the relaxation response, minis can be quite refreshing. Physically, the calming power of the minis described here comes from replacing the shallow breaths many of us normally take with abdominal breathing. This kind of breathing enhances oxygen exchange, slows your heartbeat, and lowers blood pressure. Mentally, all minirelaxation response exercises offer you a way to take a step back when you feel symptoms of stress.

Minirelaxation Reponse Exercise 1. Count down slowly from ten to zero. Take one complete breath, inhaling and then slowly exhaling, with each number. For example, breathe in deeply saying "ten" to yourself. Breathe out slowly. Say "nine" as you inhale the next breath, and so on. If you feel light-headed, count down more slowly to space your breaths further apart. When you reach zero, you should feel more relaxed. If not, go through the exercise again.

Minirelaxation Response Exercise 2. Place your hand just beneath your navel so you can feel the gentle rise and fall of your belly when you breathe. As you breathe in, count very slowly from one to four. As you breathe out, count very slowly from four down to one. Continue inhaling and exhaling slowly as you count several times or as long as you care to do so.

Minirelaxation Response Exercise 3. Sit quietly and focus on your breathing. Breathe in slowly through your nose and out through your mouth. Quietly say to yourself, "I am" as you breathe in and "at peace" as you breathe out. Repeat this phrase slowly to yourself a few times, then visualize a feeling of peace and calm.

Minirelaxation Response Exercise 4. Sit quietly and focus on your breath, breathing in slow, easy breaths down into your belly, breathing in a feeling of peace and relaxation, and breathing out tension or stress. Think of a box. It can be any size, any color. Take any worries or concerns—anything you might be anxious about—and put them in the box. Close the box and put it safely

43

on a shelf. Remember you can take the box down at any time, but right now you can leave it safely on the shelf. Breathe in and out slowly. Each time you breathe in, inhale peace. Each time you breathe out, let go of tension or discomfort. Feel yourself settling into a quiet center. Continue for another moment. Now, slowly bring yourself back to the room, knowing you can return to this quiet place at any time.

Good times to do minis are when you're stuck in traffic, are on hold during a call, or are sitting in your doctor's waiting room. They can also help when someone says something that bothers you or when you get held up standing in line.

Dealing with Cognitive Distortions

Now that you've learned some tools for eliciting the relaxation response, you're well on your way to deflating those snowballing negative thoughts we call cognitive distortions.

Cognitive therapy is built on the premise that thoughts and perceptions shape moods and emotions. If you feel depressed and anxious, your stream of thought tends to be highly negative. These negative thoughts are often riddled with distortions and exaggerations. They can be examined and deflated though, once you learn the skills of cognitive restructuring, a therapeutic technique that helps people change the way they think.

Cognitive restructuring helps you identify and challenge overly simplistic, negative thoughts that can cause unnecessary distress; for example, "This always happens to me." The following four-step process, taught at the M/BMI, is one way to help derail stress that stems from distortions and negative thoughts:

1. **Stop.** Consciously call a time-out, thus stopping the stress cycle in its tracks.
2. **Breathe.** Slowly take a few deep breaths to release physical tension and help you relax.

3. **Reflect.** Ask yourself the following questions: What are my automatic thoughts? Are these thoughts true? Am I jumping to conclusions? What evidence do I actually have? Am I letting my negative thoughts escalate? Is there another way to view the situation? What is the worst that could happen? Does it help me to think this way? Is this situation worth getting this upset about?

4. **Choose.** Learn to challenge your cognitive distortions. Ask yourself how else you can think about this situation and what else you can do to cope better with this situation. Try to see the situation differently, in a more positive light. For example, "I can handle this," "I'm doing the best I can," or "I'll get through this." Learn to choose your battles.

Challenging the way you think takes practice. Try to keep track of the situations that make you feel stressed. Apply this four-step process to help you learn to manage stress better. You needn't ignore reality or put on an artificially happy face. It's often possible to shift your focus toward the positive rather than dwelling on the negative. At other times, you can acknowledge a painful truth without losing sight of the larger, more positive picture. For example, when an illness flares up and leaves you feeling hopeless, it may help to acknowledge this without allowing it to engulf you. Change "I'll never get any better" to "I feel sick and in pain today, but I can handle this. I'm doing the best I can, and I have tools to help me cope with these symptoms. Next week, I'll probably feel better and be able to follow my normal schedule."

A common example of automatic thinking we see in people with hypertension is "My blood pressure will always be this high. I'll never get it under control, and I'm doomed to have hypertension and be on these medications forever." Instead, try saying, "It's just one blood pressure reading; it's no big deal. I can handle this. I'm doing the best I can. I'll do a minirelaxation response exercise and then recheck my blood pressure later."

Forty-One Strategies for Optimal Self-Care

The following are just a few suggestions for coping with everyday stress. Try some and see what works for you.

1. Start your day with breakfast.
2. Occasionally change your routine by meeting a friend or coworker for breakfast. Allow time to relax and enjoy it.
3. Avoid drinking coffee all day.
4. Wear comfortable clothing.
5. Find some time during the day to meditate or listen to a relaxation tape.
6. Organize your work; set priorities.
7. Don't try to be perfect. Don't feel like you have to do everything.
8. Don't try to do two, three, or more things at a time.
9. Reduce the noise level in your environment, if possible.
10. Speak up about petty annoyances while respecting others' feelings.
11. Develop a coworker support network.
12. Don't take your job home or on breaks with you.
13. Always take a lunch break (preferably not at your desk).
14. Optimize your health with good nutrition, sleep, and relaxation.
15. Get regular exercise.
16. Collaborate with coworkers to develop your own brand of happy hour, parties, birthday celebrations, and other events that act as a break in the work routine.
17. Look at unavoidable stress as an avenue for growth and change.
18. Avoid people who are "stress carriers."
19. Avoid people who are "negaholics."
20. Don't watch the news before going to bed.
21. Give yourself "praise strokes." For example, compliment yourself for a job well done.

22. Develop a wide variety of resources for gratification in your life, whether it's family, friends, hobbies, interests, special weekends, or vacations. Treat yourself to new and good things.

23. Be assertive. Learn to express your needs and differences, to make requests, and to say "no" constructively.

24. Don't overlook the emotional resources that are close at hand—coworkers, a partner, friends, and family.

25. Don't be afraid to ask questions or ask for help.

26. Allow fifteen minutes of extra time to get to appointments.

27. Check your breathing throughout the day. Take lots of deep breaths when you feel stressed.

28. Humor is a great coping strategy. Try to find something funny in the situation.

29. Find ways to give yourself a break. Take a "mental health day."

30. Adopt a pet.

31. Practice being patient. Create patience practice periods, like when waiting in line.

32. Understand that we do not all see or do things in the same way.

33. Practice mindfulness; learn to live in the moment.

34. Become a less aggressive driver.

35. Create helping rituals—they make you feel good. Open a door for someone, pick up litter, and so on.

36. When you're stressed, ask yourself, "Is this really important? Will this really matter a year from now?"

37. Resist the urge to judge or criticize.

38. Become a better listener.

39. Breathe before speaking; then you won't interrupt or finish others' sentences.

40. Be flexible with change; things don't always go as we planned.

41. Pray—speak to God, a higher power, or your inner guide.

Taking the Sting Out of Ten Common Stressors

Sometimes just thinking about embarking on a program of stress management can be stressful. Rather than freeze in your tracks, start small and bask in the glow of your successes. Give yourself a week to focus on practical solutions that can help you cope with just one stumbling block or source of stress in your life. Are you frequently late? Often irritated? Routinely juggling too many commitments? Pick a problem, and see if these suggestions work for you.

1. **Frequently late?** Apply time management principles. Consider your priorities (be sure to include time for yourself) and delegate or discard unnecessary tasks. Map out your day, segment by segment, setting aside time for different tasks, such as writing bills or making phone calls. If you are overly optimistic about travel time, consistently give yourself an extra fifteen minutes or more to get to your destinations. If lateness stems from dragging your heels, consider the underlying issue. Are you anxious about what will happen after you get to work or to a social event, for example? Or maybe you're trying to jam too many tasks into too little time.

2. **Often angry or irritated?** Consider the weight of cognitive distortions. Are you magnifying a problem or jumping to conclusions? Take the time to stop, breathe, reflect, and choose.

3. **Unsure of your ability to do something?** Don't try to go it alone. If the problem is work, talk to a coworker or supportive boss. Ask a knowledgeable friend or call the local library or an organization that can supply the information you need. Write down other ways that you might get the answers or skills you require. Turn to tapes, books, or classes, for example, if you need a little tutelage. This works equally well when you're learning relaxation response techniques.

4. **Overextended?** Clear the deck of at least one time-consuming household task. Hire a cleaning service, shop for groceries on the Internet, convene a family meeting to consider who can take on certain jobs, or barter with or pay teens for work around the house and yard. Consider what is truly essential and important to you and what can take a backseat right now.

5. **Not enough time for stress relief?** Try minirelaxation response exercises. Or make a commitment to yourself to pare down your schedule for just one week so you can practice the relaxation response every day. Slowing down to pay attention to just one task or pleasure is an excellent method of stress relief.

6. **Feeling unbearably tense?** Try massage or self-massage, a hot bath, minirelaxation response exercises, progressive muscle relaxation, or a mindful walk. Practically any exercise—a brisk walk, a quick run, a sprint up and down the stairs—will help too. Done regularly, exercise wards off tension, as do relaxation response techniques.

7. **Frequently pessimistic?** Remind yourself of the value of learned optimism—a more joyful life and, quite possibly, better health. Practice deflating cognitive distortions. Rent funny movies and read amusing books. Create a mental list of things for which you feel grateful. If the list seems too short, consider beefing up your social network and adding creative, productive, and leisure pursuits to your life.

8. **Upset by conflicts with others?** State your needs or distress directly, avoiding "you always" or "you never" zingers. Use "I feel _____ when you _____"; "I would really appreciate it if you could _____"; and "I need some help setting priorities. What needs to be done first and what should I tackle later?" If conflicts are a significant source of distress for you, consider taking a class in assertiveness training.

9. **Worn out or burned out?** Focus on self-nurturing techniques. Carve out time to practice the relaxation

response or at least indulge in minirelaxation response exercises. Care for your body by eating good, healthy food and for your heart by seeking out others. Consider your priorities in life: Is it worth feeling this way, or is another path open to you? If you want help, consider what kind would be best. Do you want a job taken off your hands? Do you want to do it at a later date? Do you need someone with particular expertise to assist you?

10. **Feeling lonely?** Connect with others. Even little connections—a brief conversation while in line at the grocery store, an exchange about local goings-on with a neighbor, a question for a colleague—can help melt the ice within you. It also may embolden you to seek more opportunities to connect. Be a volunteer. Attend religious or community functions. Suggest coffee with an acquaintance. Call a friend or relative you miss. Take an interesting class. If social phobias, low self-esteem, or depression are dampening your desire to reach out, seek help. The world is a kinder, more wondrous place when you share its pleasures and burdens.

Next Steps

You've learned some excellent tools in this chapter, but remember that a tool is only as useful as your ability and willingness to use it when it's needed. Knowing what to do is not enough, and that fact alone is probably your greatest challenge in learning to manage your stress. Stress management is a skill. It will take practice, just like learning to ride a bicycle. And just as in learning to ride a bicycle, you're likely to wobble and fall from time to time, just like all of us. The more you practice, the easier it gets. When practiced, your new stress management skills will become a key weapon in battling hypertension. But as you're about to learn, there's even more you can do. In the next two chapters we'll take a look at how diet and exercise can and should be part of your program. We'll cover healthful eating first.

CHAPTER 4

DASHing Your Way to Healthier Blood Pressure

How strange our culture is when it comes to diet. For all the attention we give the topic, you'd think that most of us would fare better. At any given time, it seems, at least one popular diet book has a foothold high on the *New York Times* bestseller list. Millions of dollars are spent yearly on diet products, diet books, diet programs, and modified (low-carb and low-fat) foods. Yet, as a culture, we consistently display among the worst diet habits in the world, and it shows. A full two-thirds of Americans are now considered overweight or obese, due almost entirely to poor diet and lack of exercise (which we'll discuss in the next chapter).

When it comes to eating, many people with hypertension envision a regimen of near-military rigidity: absolutely no salt, limp vegetables, tofu, wheat germ, seaweed, and other "healthy" foods. It's all too easy to get confused. Not long ago, a "balanced diet" meant dividing your plate evenly between the meat group and the potatoes group. Nowadays, the common wisdom is quite different, and it's not always easy to distinguish the latest scientific research from the latest marketing campaign by the diet guru du jour.

But after decades of study, scientists have concluded that the typical American diet is a recipe for hypertension and cardiovascular disease: too much salt, too much saturated fat, too many calories, and not enough fruits, vegetables, and whole grains. You know that your diet has a profound effect on your health and well-being. The food choices you make throughout each day are actually the choices you make about how you look and feel and about your long-term health.

A healthy diet, along with regular exercise, has the power to help prevent heart disease and hypertension. As you'll discover in this chapter, eating to control hypertension also means feeling great and eating well—with no shortage of food options. You'll also learn about the Dietary Approaches to Stopping Hypertension, also known as *DASH*. Our discussion includes, as any discussion about diet should, a solid foundation of nutritional know-how, followed by a step-by-step plan to lower your blood pressure, take off extra pounds, and leave your body energized and vibrant.

Now DASH Away, DASH Away, DASH Away All

In a landmark study conducted in 1997, 459 men and women with hypertension (classified then as higher than 140/90 mm/Hg) were randomly assigned to follow one of three diets: their normal diet, a diet rich in fruits and vegetables, or the so-called DASH diet. The people in the fruit-and-vegetable diet saw their blood pressure drop, but those on the DASH diet saw it drop even more. The effects of the DASH plan were swift, with blood pressure dropping significantly after just two weeks; after following the plan for eight weeks, study participants enjoyed average reductions of 11.4 mm/Hg in systolic pressure and 5.5 mm/Hg in diastolic pressure. These results are comparable to the effects of some antihypertensive medicines.

The DASH diet cut blood pressure so dramatically that the researchers concluded that it may reduce or sometimes eliminate the need for medication. For people already on medication, the diet may enable them to reduce the dose or the number of medications they are taking. These findings persuaded the Joint National Committee on Prevention, Detection, Evaluation, and Treatment of High Blood Pressure (JNC 7)—the government organization that issues guidelines on blood pressure treatment—to recommend the DASH diet (along with weight loss and reduced salt intake) as a means of preventing and treating hypertension.

It seems that starting on the DASH diet is like flipping a blood pressure–lowering switch in the body. So how does this revolutionary eating plan differ from the way you may presently be eating? One distinguishing feature of this diet is the strong emphasis it places on fruit and vegetable consumption. In fact, when the DASH diet is represented as a pyramid, as in Figure 4.1, vegeta-

FIGURE 4.1 DASH Pyramid

What's in a serving:
1 Tbsp sugar, 1 Tbsp jelly or jam, ½ oz jelly beans, 8 oz lemonade

What's in a serving:
1 tsp soft margarine, 1 Tbsp low-fat mayonnaise, 2 Tbsp light salad dressing, 1 tsp vegetable oil

What's in a serving:
⅓ cup nuts, 2 Tbsp seeds, ½ cup cooked beans or peas

What's in a serving:
3 oz cooked meat, poultry, or fish

What's in a serving:
8 oz milk, 1 cup yogurt, 1½ oz cheese

What's in a serving:
1 slice bread; 1 oz dry cereal; ½ cup cooked rice, pasta, or cereal

Sweets
(5 per week)

Nuts, seeds, and beans
(4–5 per week)

Fats and oils
(2–3 per day)

Low-fat dairy
(2–3 per day)

Meats, poultry, and fish
(2 or fewer per day)

Grains
(preferably whole)
(7–8 per day)

Vegetables and fruits
(8–10 per day)

What's in a serving:
1 medium fruit; 6 oz fruit juice; ½ cup fresh, frozen, or canned fruit; ¼ cup dried fruit

What's in a serving:
1 cup raw leafy vegetable, ½ cup cooked vegetable, 6 oz vegetable juice

Adapted from the National Institute of Health's DASH Eating Plan, nhlbi.nih.gov/health/public/heart/hbp/dash and fruits form the base. The pyramid shows the foods you should eat the most of at the bottom and the least of at the top, with all the other food groups ranged in between. The DASH diet also encourages the consumption of whole grains versus refined starches and low-fat dairy products instead of their higher-fat counterparts. Nuts and good fats from oily fish, olive oil, and canola oil are also recommended.

When it comes to following any food guide, deciphering servings can be a little confusing. The DASH plan, for example, calls for eight to ten servings of fruits and vegetables per day. What's a serving? How large should one apple be? How many grapes or blueberries make up the serving equivalent of a banana or grapefruit? To make things easier, the DASH serving sizes have been broken down into easily measurable portions and the number of servings clearly spelled out. Table 4.1 shows examples and serving measurements for each food group.

TABLE 4.1 Food Group Servings and the DASH Diet

Food Group	Daily Servings	Serving Sizes	Examples	Significance to the DASH Diet
Grains and grain products	7–8	1 slice bread 1 ounce dry cereal ½ cup cooked rice, pasta, or cereal	Whole-wheat bread, English muffins, pita bread, bagels, cereals, grits, oatmeal	Major sources of energy and fiber
Vegetables	4–5	1 cup raw leafy vegetable ½ cup cooked vegetable 6 ounces vegetable juice	Tomatoes, potatoes, carrots, peas, squash, broccoli, turnip greens, collards, kale, spinach, artichokes, beans, sweet potatoes	Rich sources of potassium, magnesium, and fiber
Fruits	4–5	6 ounces fruit juice 1 medium fruit ¼ cup dried fruit ½ cup fresh, frozen, or canned fruit	Apricots, bananas, dates, grapefruit, mangoes, melons, oranges, peaches, pineapples, prunes, raisins, strawberries, tangerines	Important sources of potassium, magnesium, and fiber

Food Group	Daily Servings	Serving Sizes	Examples	Significance to the DASH Diet
Low-fat or nonfat dairy foods	2–3	8 ounces milk 1 cup yogurt 1½ ounces cheese	Skim or 1% milk, skim or low-fat buttermilk, nonfat or low-fat yogurt, nonfat or low-fat cheese	Major sources of calcium and protein
Meats, poultry, and fish	2 or fewer	3 ounces cooked meat, poultry, or fish	Select only lean; trim away visible fats; broil, roast, or boil instead of frying; remove skin from poultry	Rich sources of protein and magnesium
Nuts, seeds, and beans	4–5 per week	1½ ounces or ⅓ cup nuts ½ ounce or 2 tablespoons seeds ½ cup cooked legumes	Almonds, filberts, mixed nuts, peanuts, walnuts, sunflower seeds, kidney beans, lentils	Rich sources of energy, magnesium, potassium, protein, and fiber
Fats and oils	2–3	1 teaspoon vegetable oil 1 tablespoon low-fat mayonnaise 2 tablespoons light salad dressing	Margarine, low-fat mayonnaise, light salad dressing, vegetable oil (olive, canola, corn, or safflower)	DASH has 27% of calories as fat, including fat in or added to foods
Sweets	5 per week	1 tablespoon sugar 8 ounces lemonade 1 tablespoon jelly or jam	Maple syrup, sugar, jelly, jam, fruit-flavored gelatin, hard candy, sorbet	Should be low in fat

Source: Dietary Approaches to Stop Hypertension (DASH) study, National Institutes of Health, nhlbi.nih.gov, 2003.

You'll notice that the number of daily or weekly servings can vary. Unless you eat exactly the same things in the same portions every day, you're likely to—as most people do—eat more of some foods on some days and less on others. That's fine. Just try to make your overall consumption from each food group average out over the course of, say, a week to the proper servings and portion sizes. Check Appendix B for some DASH-friendly recipes that are very tasty and simple to make.

Looking for Hidden Salt

An adult requires only about 250 milligrams (mg) of sodium a day, but most Americans consume at least 3,300 mg a day. As previously mentioned, many health organizations recommend that people keep their intake below 2,300 mg a day and below 1,500 to 2,000 mg for older adults, African Americans (who are at a statistically higher risk for hypertension), and people with hypertension and heart disease. Salt causes your body to retain fluid, which increases the volume of blood in your circulatory system. That means that your heart has to work harder to do its job, causing your blood pressure to increase.

You might be surprised to learn that only 15 percent of the salt you eat comes from your salt shaker. In fact, the vast majority—about 75 percent—of the excess salt in the typical American diet lurks hidden in many manufactured or processed foods you buy at the store. Soups (canned, dried, or frozen), lunch meats, cold cereals, frozen dinners, salad dressings, cheese, pizza, bread and rolls, crackers, olives, pickles, cured meats, kosher meats, hot dogs, potato chips, corn chips, pretzels, and nuts—all of them are almost always teeming with blood-pressure-raising amounts of salt. (The remaining 10 percent of the salt you ingest occurs naturally in certain foods such as meat, milk, and some vegetables.)

Some popular frozen dinners packaged as "healthy," "smart," or "lean" choices often have more than half the sodium (up to about 700 mg) your body needs for an entire day. Read labels on snacks, cereals, and frozen dinners to find out how much salt they contain. Here's a good rule to follow: if it comes in a can, a box, a bag, or a jar, check the back to see how much salt might be hiding there. Good choices would be snack-type foods with less than 200 mg sodium per serving and meal-type foods (frozen entrees, soups, burger patties, and so on) with less than 500 mg sodium per serving. Table 4.2 shows some simple low-sodium alternatives to common food items.

Other sources of salt include the seasonings you may add to your foods, including seasoned salt (garlic, onion, and celery salts,

TABLE 4.2 List of High-Sodium Foods/Brand Names and Their Low-Sodium Alternatives

High-Sodium Foods	Low-Sodium Alternatives
Most canned soups	Amy's Organic, Healthy Choice, Campbell's, and Progresso low-sodium soups
Cheddar cheese, American cheese	Swiss cheese (Alpine Lace), Laughing Cow Light wedges, Cabot 50% and 75% light cheddar cheese
Soup bouillon cubes	Herbox Very Low Sodium Soup mix
Canned vegetables	Fresh and frozen vegetables
Soy sauce	Tamari (low-sodium natural soy sauce), Kikkoman Light Soy Sauce
Most frozen entrees	Cascadian Farms, Spa Cuisine
Regular canned tomatoes, tomato sauce	No-added-salt canned tomatoes (Hunt's, store brand)
Regular cottage cheese	Hood No Added Salt Light Cottage Cheese
Ragu/Prego/Classico marinara sauce	Trader Joe's No-Added-Salt Organic Marinara
Regular salt or sea salt	Morton Lite salt, Mrs. Dash seasoning blends
Corn Flakes, Froot Loops	Kashi Go Lean, most Kashi cereals
Ritz crackers, saltines	Wasa crispbread, Kavli, Ak-Mak crackers
Regular salsa	Trader Joe's low-sodium salsa
Deli turkey	Thanksgiving style turkey (available at most grocery stores in deli section)
Regular seasoning sauces, marinades, and salad dressings	Mrs. Dash no-added-salt sauces, marinades, and dressings

for example), baking powder, baking soda, soy sauce, steak sauce, Worcestershire sauce, and monosodium glutamate.

Alcohol: Friend or Foe?

Some research has indicated that alcohol may have some heart-healthy effects. Some studies say that certain chemicals found in red wine may have antioxidant properties and may raise high-density lipoproteins (HDL), or "good" cholesterol. Then there's the other set of studies that concluded that it's not just wine but any type of alcohol that may be heart-healthy due to its blood

Ten Tips to Reduce the Salt in Your Diet

1. The taste buds that are sensitive to salt are also sensitive to acid, so you can "fool" them with convenient salt alternatives. Leave the salt shaker off the table and replace it with a bowl of lemon wedges; squeeze them over your food. Also, avoid using salt while cooking; use lime juice, lemon juice, vinegars, Mrs. Dash seasonings, lite salt (half the sodium as regular salt), or salt substitute (potassium chloride) instead.

2. Buy vegetables that are fresh, frozen, or canned "with no salt added."

3. Use fresh poultry, fish, and lean meat, rather than canned or processed types.

4. Use herbs, spices, and salt-free seasoning blends in cooking and at the table.

5. Cook rice, pasta, and hot cereals without salt. Cut back on instant or flavored rice, pasta, and cereal mixes, as well as on other salty foods such as cheeses, pickles, deli meats, and olives.

6. Choose convenience foods that are lower in sodium. Cut back on frozen dinners, packaged mixes, canned soups or broths, and salad dressings.

7. Rinse canned foods, such as beans and tuna, to remove some sodium.

8. When available, buy low-sodium, reduced-sodium, or no-salt-added versions of foods.

9. Choose breakfast cereals that are lower in sodium.

10. Snack on fruits and vegetables instead of chips.

thinning effect. What all these studies have in common, however, is the finding that only moderate amounts of alcohol may have any benefit. Heavy drinking, on the other hand, increases blood pressure and triglycerides, not to mention weight, and interferes with blood pressure medication. Moderate alcohol use for men is defined as no more than two drinks (two ounces of alcohol) a day.

However, women absorb more alcohol than men and should limit their daily intake to one drink (one ounce of alcohol) per day. Small or underweight people are more susceptible to the effects of alcohol than heavier people and should consume no more than half an ounce daily.

The following drinks contain about an ounce of alcohol:

- One ounce of 100-proof liquor
- One and a half ounces (a jigger) of 80-proof liquor (bourbon, gin, rum, scotch, tequila, vodka, or whiskey)
- Three ounces of fortified wine (sherry, port, marsala, or Madeira)
- Four to five ounces of table wine
- Twelve ounces of regular or light beer

Aside from the alcohol content, keep an eye on those calories. Even a bottle of light beer has about 100 calories, and other drinks, such as a frozen mudslide, really pack in the calories and fat.

Shed the Pounds, Lower the Numbers

If you're more than 10 percent over your ideal weight, you may be able to reduce your blood pressure significantly through weight loss. According to the JNC 7 report, you can reduce your systolic blood pressure by 1 mm/Hg for every two pounds you lose.

So what exactly *is* your ideal weight? Determining that isn't as straightforward as reading the numbers on your bathroom scale. To figure out whether you're at a healthy weight, you'll need to calculate your body mass index (BMI). Your BMI is a number that represents your proportion of weight to height. Two hundred pounds might be a great weight for a six-foot male athlete but alarming for a sedentary man who's only five foot five.

To estimate your BMI, take a look at Table 4.3. First, identify your height (to the nearest inch) in the far left column of the chart. Next, move your finger across the row corresponding to that height until you come to the column that represents your

TABLE 4.3 Figuring Body Mass Index

BMI (kg/m²)	19	20	21	22	23	24	25	26	27	28	29	30	35	40
Height (in.)							Weight (lb.)							
58	91	96	100	105	110	115	119	124	129	134	138	143	167	191
59	94	99	104	109	114	119	124	128	133	138	143	148	173	198
60	97	102	107	112	118	123	128	133	138	143	148	153	179	204
61	100	106	111	116	122	127	132	137	143	148	153	158	185	211
62	104	109	115	120	126	131	136	142	147	153	158	164	191	218
63	107	113	118	124	130	135	141	146	152	158	163	169	197	225
64	110	116	122	128	134	140	145	151	157	163	169	174	204	232
65	114	120	126	132	138	144	150	156	162	168	174	180	210	240
66	118	124	130	136	142	148	155	161	167	173	179	186	216	247
67	121	127	134	140	146	153	159	166	172	178	185	191	223	255
68	125	131	138	144	151	158	164	171	177	184	190	197	230	262
69	128	135	142	149	155	162	169	176	182	189	196	203	236	270
70	132	139	146	153	160	167	174	181	188	195	202	207	243	278
71	136	143	150	157	165	172	179	186	193	200	208	215	250	286
72	140	147	154	162	169	177	184	191	199	206	213	221	258	294
73	144	151	159	166	174	182	189	197	204	212	219	227	265	302
74	148	155	163	171	179	186	194	202	210	218	225	233	272	311
75	152	160	168	176	184	192	200	208	216	224	232	240	279	319
76	156	164	172	180	189	197	205	213	221	230	238	246	287	328

weight (to the closest pound). The number at the top of that column is your BMI.

A BMI of 19 to 24 is considered healthy, whereas a BMI of 25 to 29 is defined as overweight. Obesity begins at a BMI of 30. You should keep in mind that, even though BMI is very useful, looking at these numbers alone can be somewhat deceptive. That's because BMI can overestimate the level of risk in people who are muscular (such as athletes), who may be overweight according to the BMI chart but still have a high level of lean muscle mass and a low level of body fat. These individuals would still be considered healthy. On the other hand, in individuals who may be normal weight but have a higher level of body fat and a lower level of lean muscle mass, using just BMI as a risk indicator would underestimate the level of risk. In general, a body fat percentage level of 11–22 percent in men and 23–33 percent in women is considered normal.

Let's assume that you have a BMI that's just above the healthy range, and you'd like to take off a couple of pounds—make it five. Where do you begin? First, there's something very important that anybody who wants to lose weight needs to understand. For all the popular diets and nutritional products on the market today, one basic physiological fact remains: the only way to lose weight is to burn more calories through a combination of metabolism (the calories burned just to keep your body working) and physical activity than you take in through food and drink. There is no other safe, healthy way to lose weight. That said, the principal behind weight loss becomes much more simple and direct than any low-carb, no-carb, or other fad diet out there. Weight loss is like accounting—every time you eat, you're making a "deposit" into your calorie bank. Unless you make a "withdrawal" (in the form of either calorie reduction or exercise or both), your deposit will stay put and even gain "interest" in the form of contributing to low energy, poor body image, high blood pressure, and other potential problems. If you want to lose weight, either increase your activity or reduce your total calories or both—it's as simple as that.

Let's go back to those five pounds. Research suggests that one to two pounds is the maximum amount of weight that a person can lose safely within a week. But that may be a little ambitious. It would take some pretty strict calorie cutting and some long, intense exercise sessions to accomplish that. So let's make it a little more feasible. Let's say that you'll aim at losing one-half pound a week for ten weeks. Some weeks you may lose more; some weeks you may lose less. But at the end of ten weeks, you'll be five pounds lighter.

One pound of excess body fat is the equivalent of 3,500 calories that were eaten but not used up. In order to lose one-half pound a week, you'll need to cut 1,750 calories from your diet, or 250 calories per day. That's not hard at all! If you're one of the many Americans who drink a 20-ounce bottle of soda every day, simply cutting that out would be almost enough to reach your goal. This is assuming that you are not currently gaining weight. Cutting 250 calories from a 3,500-calorie-a-day diet will do little more than slightly slow down your weight gain. To lose weight, these calories must be cut from a stable intake of 1,800 to 2,000 daily calories for the average woman and 2,200 to 2,500 daily calories for the average man. If you're currently consuming more than this, then you'll need to cut more calories from your diet.

In the next chapter we'll talk about how exercise can supplement or help with weight loss. That is, if you burn calories through exercise in addition to cutting an average 250 calories from your daily eating you'll lose even more than half a pound per week. You can also opt to cut 125 calories a day from eating and burn another 125 calories through exercise to reach the same calorie balance required to lose that one-half pound. (Again, it's all about balancing calories in and calories out.) But for now, let's look at some more ways to cut a simple 250 calories from your daily eating.

You don't necessarily have to give up certain foods completely, but you can make sensible reductions and substitutions throughout the day; Table 4.4 contains some helpful suggestions. Assuming you're like most Americans who eat five times per day (three meals and two snacks), you'll need only to lose 50 calories each time you eat—you'll hardly know you're dieting.

Often it is not *what* you eat but *how* you eat that can be a key factor in weight loss. As a culture, we are always in a rush, and this spills over into how we eat as well. Fast-food meals have replaced sit-down mealtimes, and even the practice of eating while driving has become such a cultural phenomenon that the term *dashboard dining* has been coined to describe it. The problem with eating mindlessly and fast is that you may end up eating more than you would if you slowed down, savored each bite, and paid attention to how much you were eating. There's a scientific reason behind this. It takes twenty minutes from the time you start eating for the "fullness signal" in the brain to be activated. That means that if you took about twenty minutes to eat your meal,

TABLE 4.4 Healthy Substitutions

Instead of	Try
Cream in your coffee	Half-and-half (good), whole milk (better), low-fat milk (best)
Donut/bagel for breakfast	2 slices whole-wheat bread with 1 tablespoon peanut butter
Sweetened fruit yogurt	Plain nonfat yogurt with chopped fruit added
Canned fruit	Fresh fruit
Candy	Dried fruit
Granola bar	Handful of whole-grain cereal (such as Cheerios) with a few nuts and dried fruit
Regular potato chips/corn chips	Baked chips
Cheez-its or Triscuits	Ak-Mak or reduced-fat Triscuits
American cheese	Low-fat cheese (try Cabot 50% light or Kraft 2% Singles)
Butter	Low-fat or trans fat–free margarine (Promise Lite, Brummel and Brown)
Regular soda	Seltzer with lime, diet soda
Cream cheese	Low-fat cream cheese, hummus
Half-and-half	Fat-free half-and-half
Delivery pizza	Delivery pizza with half the cheese
Butter on vegetables or potatoes	Butter Buds, Molly McButter (spice aisle)
Fried chicken/fish	Oven-fried chicken/fish
French fries	Oven-baked fries
Parmesan cheese	Fat-free Parmesan or "veggie" Parmesan
Iced cake	Angel food cake

you could actually end up being satisfied with a smaller portion of food, not to mention that you would probably end up enjoying the food more and be less likely to get indigestion afterward. Some other behavioral changes that may help with weight loss are as follows:

- Eat from a smaller plate. We tend to fill our plates with more food when we eat from big plates.
- Start your meal with a hot beverage, such as hot tea, soup, or broth. Hot liquids are more filling than cold liquids and may help you eat less during the meal.
- Don't surround yourself with temptations. Go out and get a scoop of ice cream once in a while when you feel like you

really want it, instead of keeping cartons of ice cream in the freezer.

- Portion out snacks ahead of time instead of snacking right from the box.
- Fill up your plate once and avoid taking second helpings. If you still feel slightly hungry at the end of the meal, have a piece of fruit instead.
- Ask yourself whether you are truly hungry before you snack. Sometimes anxiety, boredom, loneliness, and even thirst can make you reach for food. Drink a glass of water and see whether it satisfies you. Stop before you reach for a snack, take a deep breath, and be aware of your mood. See whether you can outlast the urge to snack or find other means to relax if you are stressed, such as going for a walk or calling a friend.

No doubt about it: calories should be the number-one focus when it comes to losing or maintaining weight. But calories and body weight aren't the only things to consider when creating a healthy diet. You already know that too much salt can have ill effects on your health. Let's take a look at some of the other things you'll want to pay attention to as part of your heart-healthy eating plan in order to reduce blood pressure, achieve or maintain a healthy weight, and enjoy overall good health.

Cholesterol: The Good and the Bad

Cholesterol is a type of lipid (fat) that your body uses for many things. It is a building block of cell membranes, the critically important "skin" that surrounds cells. It is used to make the bile acids that help us digest and absorb food. Cholesterol is also an important precursor to vitamin D and a number of hormones, including testosterone and estrogen. In fact, cholesterol is so important for proper functioning that our bodies regulate its level in the blood—called *serum cholesterol* or *blood cholesterol*—by producing cholesterol on their own when our diet alone does not supply enough. Nutritionists use the words *dietary cholesterol* to distinguish the kind we eat from the kind our bodies manufacture. Most people's bodies already make more cholesterol than they need, and they could stand to cut back on foods that boost cholesterol levels, such as those high in saturated fats and trans fats.

The bloodstream is the distribution channel for delivering a steady supply of cholesterol and other lipids to all the cells in your body. This process isn't as simple as it sounds. Like oil and water, lipids and blood don't mix. To get around this problem, the body packages fat into proteinlike particles that mix easily with blood and flow with it. These tiny particles are called *lipoproteins* (*lipid* plus *protein*).

- **Low-density lipoproteins (the bad guys).** Virtually all cells in the body can take up and use low-density lipoproteins (LDL) for their individual cholesterol needs. But because there are usually more LDL particles in circulation at any one time than your body can use, it's your liver's job to clear the excess from the blood and use it to make more bile acids or new lipoproteins. If the liver can't keep up with the supply of LDL, these particles can come to rest in the wrong places, typically in the lining of blood vessels, which makes them unhealthy for your heart. For LDL, levels of 130 mg/dL or above would be considered high for people at risk for heart disease. For people with heart disease, 100 mg/dL or above is considered high, although the latest studies suggest that people with an LDL level below 70 mg/dL have the lowest mortality rates and lowest incidence of heart attack or stroke.
- **High-density lipoproteins (the good guys).** HDL, the "good" cholesterol made by the liver and intestines, resembles LDL only in its acronym. It looks and behaves quite differently from LDL. HDL particles, by definition, have lots of protein but not much fat. They sponge up excess

cholesterol from the linings of blood vessels and elsewhere and carry it off to the liver. If you think of the LDL that builds up inside blood vessels as circulatory garbage, then HDL is like a garbage collector that picks up fatty materials from blood vessel walls and delivers them to the liver for removal. HDL levels of less than 40 mg/dL in men and less than 50 mg/dL in women are regarded as low and a risk factor for heart disease. Levels of 60 mg/dL or above are considered exceptionally good.

- **Triglycerides.** Much of the noncholesterol fat found in lipoprotein particles is triglycerides. The name comes from the structure: three fatty acids bound to an alcohol called *glycerol*. Triglycerides are essential for good health because your tissues rely on them for energy. Too much triglyceride seems to be bad for the arteries and the heart. The guidelines for triglyceride levels say that below 150 mg/dL is normal, 150 to 199 mg/dL is borderline high, 200 to 499 mg/dL is high, and 500 mg/dL and above is very high.
- **Total cholesterol.** Total cholesterol is the sum of cholesterol carried in all the lipoproteins (LDL, HDL, and triglycerides) in the blood. A total cholesterol level below 200 mg/dL is desirable, 200 to 239 mg/dL is borderline high, and 240 mg/dL and above is high.

The Other Players

Many other food components play a role in the nutritional value of your meals. The amount of fats, carbohydrates, protein, fiber, potassium, calcium, and magnesium you ingest can influence how well your body uses food and what gets stored as fat cells.

Fats

Contrary to conventional wisdom, not all fats are bad. For many years, fat and health seemed as incompatible as oil and water. A prerequisite for making your diet healthier was to cut fat down to

no more than 30 percent of your daily calories—the less
ter. Cookbook authors, diet programs, and the media all ju
on the low-fat bandwagon.

The alternative view, held for decades by many leaders in
nutrition research, was that the key to heart health was the *type*,
not the *amount*, of fat; this view turned out to be correct. Fat is a
major energy source for your body and also helps you absorb certain vitamins and nutrients. You can get up to 25–35 percent of
your calories from fat and still have a diet that's good for your
heart, helps reduce your risk of hypertension, and lets you maintain or even lose weight. But here's the catch: these fats must be
the "good" type. Unfortunately for lovers of red meat, butter, and
cheese, these foods don't qualify and should be avoided or limited
to occasional treats. Confused about whether a fat is good or bad?
Table 4.5 outlines the differences.

Saturated fats from foods should be limited to less than 7 percent of total calorie intake, or less than 15 to 20 grams a day. Cholesterol should be limited to 200 mg a day or less, which is about
the amount in one egg yolk.

TABLE 4.5 Distinguishing Good and Bad Fats

Good Fats			Bad Fats	
Monounsaturated (do not raise LDL, do not lower HDL)	Polyunsaturated		Saturated (may raise LDL and lower HDL)	Trans (may raise LDL and lower HDL)
Canola oil	Omega-6s (do not raise LDL, may lower HDL)	Omega-3s (have blood-thinning properties, may lower triglycerides)	Full-fat dairy products (butter, whole milk, etc.)	Margarine with hydrogenated oils
Olive oil	Corn oil	Oily fish	Red meat (beef, veal, lamb, pork)	Deep-fried foods (donuts, etc.)
Nut oils, nuts, nut butters	Vegetable oil	Flaxseeds	Coconut, coconut oil, palm kernel oil	Crackers, cookies, chips, popcorn
Avocados		Walnuts		

It is important to remember that fats are classified as good or bad based on the effect they have on your cholesterol levels and heart. But when it comes to their effect on weight, all fats have the same effect: they all have nine calories per gram.

Carbohydrates

Carbohydrates come in a broad range of foods, including table sugar, fruits and vegetables, and grains such as rice and wheat. They should account for 50–60 percent of your daily calories, but most of them should come from whole-grain foods, vegetables, and fruits. If most of the carbohydrates you eat come from white bread, potatoes, white rice, and refined sugar, you could end up gaining weight and putting yourself at risk for some serious diseases. The list of bad carbohydrates may come as a surprise. Why is white bread bad for you? Why is it in the same category as sweets? Why is whole-wheat bread better? To answer these questions, you have to consider the *glycemic load*, a measure of how quickly a serving of food is converted to blood sugar during digestion and how high the spike in blood sugar is. In general, the good carbohydrates (whole grains, fruits, vegetables) have a lower glycemic load than the bad carbohydrates, meaning they convert more slowly and stay with you longer. The glycemic load of your diet can significantly affect your risk for diabetes, heart disease, and, possibly, obesity.

Protein

Protein is essential for building and repairing tissue throughout the body. About 15 percent of your daily calories should come from protein. A good deal of research continues to look into whether protein from plant sources—soy, lentils, beans, and nuts—is healthier than protein from meat. While there isn't enough evidence to state that plant protein is better for you than meat protein, food sources of plant protein also tend to be lower in calories and saturated fats and higher in fiber. (And there are many more sources of nonmeat protein than most people think.

See the healthy shopping list in Appendix C for more details.) If you do eat meat for protein, eat only small portions (one serving = three ounces) and choose lean cuts.

Fiber

Fiber is a form of indigestible carbohydrate found mainly in plant foods. Over the years, fiber has been hailed as a potent weapon against colon cancer, high cholesterol, and heart disease. What's so great about it? Having lots of fiber in your diet decreases your risk of heart disease and helps prevent constipation. It also slows the digestion of foods and therefore lowers their glycemic load, possibly helping to prevent diabetes. By increasing the bulk of foods and creating a feeling of fullness, fiber may also help you avoid overeating. The goal should be to eat 25 to 40 grams of fiber per day. (On average, Americans eat only about 15 grams a day.)

You can probably identify some high-fiber foods, such as bran cereals and whole-grain bread. But not all products billed as "high fiber" really have much, so read the labels on packaged foods to see the number of grams they actually contain. You can be sure of getting fiber if you eat fruits, vegetables, and whole-grain foods such

Simple Ways to Boost Your Fiber Intake

- Eat whole-grain cereal—such as oatmeal or cereals that list whole wheat, oats, barley, or another whole grain first on the list of ingredients—for breakfast.
- Choose whole-grain breads and crackers (at least 2 grams of fiber per serving).
- Trade the French fries for sweet potatoes or yams, and swap the white rice for brown rice, kasha, bulgur, millet, quinoa, or barley.
- Try whole-wheat pizza crust and pasta instead of those made with white flour.
- Bake with whole-wheat flour.

as whole-wheat bread, brown rice, and oats each day. (See Appendix C for more options.)

Potassium

Consuming too little potassium can raise your blood pressure and your risk of stroke. A twelve-year study determined that men who consumed low amounts of potassium were 2.6 times more likely to die from stroke than men who consumed moderate to high amounts. The results were even more sobering for women. Women with the lowest potassium intake had a nearly fivefold increase in risk. In other studies, researchers induced a rise in blood pressure in both normal and hypertensive people simply by restricting potassium.

Increasing dietary potassium may allow some people to reduce the dose of their blood pressure medicine. Before increasing your potassium intake, check with your doctor. Some people—for example, those with kidney disease—may need to avoid both potassium and salt. Fruits and vegetables are good sources of potassium, which is one of the reasons they are the foundation of the DASH diet pyramid.

Calcium

Some research suggests that a low calcium intake may contribute to high blood pressure, but calcium's exact role in hypertension is unknown. One theory holds that a lack of calcium in the diet predisposes your body to retain sodium, which raises blood pressure. For this reason, it may be especially important that salt-sensitive people with hypertension get an appropriate amount of calcium.

But because many Americans simply don't get enough in their diets and calcium is vital for preventing osteoporosis, few would argue against the use of supplements to boost your calcium intake. Required daily amounts vary with age, but most adults under fifty should aim for 1,000 mg per day; those over fifty should increase their intake to 1,200 mg per day. Eating three servings a day of low-fat dairy products such as low-fat milk, yogurt, or cheese can ensure adequate calcium intake.

Magnesium

Some evidence links a low amount of dietary magnesium with hypertension, but experts aren't sure whether this mineral alone affects blood pressure or if the effect comes from other nutrients, such as calcium and potassium, often found in foods containing magnesium. Foods rich in magnesium include whole grains, nuts, beans, seeds, fish, avocado, and leafy vegetables. However, you should not take more than the dose of magnesium recommended for the general population (310 to 420 mg a day), which is generally found in a multivitamin.

Balancing Your Plate

Here's where we take everything we've learned and put it all together. In the previous section you learned a lot of technical information about a nontechnical activity: eating. Now let's put it all into terms that are easy to understand and into a plan that's easy to implement.

Here's what we know. The DASH diet is somewhat similar to the conventional food guide pyramid but differs in that it emphasizes fruits and vegetables over grains and also allows for more fats, as long as they're the healthy kind. (Sweets occupy the pyramid's capstone.) The DASH diet combined with physical activity (which we'll discuss shortly) and stress management create a powerful, balanced three-legged stool to firmly support your efforts to lower your blood pressure. The DASH diet also pays special attention to sodium intake—sodium isn't out of the question for people with hypertension, but it should be kept carefully in check.

We discussed how weight loss can help lower blood pressure and that losing weight can happen gradually, easily, and without a hard-core attitude toward dieting and exercise.

Finally, we took a look at some general dietary recommendations, including recommended portions of the healthy forms of carbohydrates, fats, and proteins, and the role other dietary players have in stabilizing or lowering your blood pressure.

All of this brings us back to those average five times a day that you eat. What should you eat and in what amounts? You'll want to refer back to Table 4.1 for examples from each food group, but the idea of balancing your plate at mealtime is simpler than you might think.

Balancing Breakfast

Aim to combine fruits with whole grains and lean protein (eggs in moderation, egg whites, nut butters, nuts, and low-fat dairy) at breakfast. For example, try a serving of oatmeal topped with half a cup of fresh blueberries and a glass of skim milk. Or two slices of whole-grain toast, a medium piece of fruit, and a glass of skim milk. You might also combine low-fat plain yogurt with berries and whole-grain cereal. (Or see Appendix B for some heart-healthy breakfast recipes.)

Balancing Dinner and Lunch

At dinner and lunch, use your plate as a visual guide, as shown in Figure 4.2. Aim to fill half of it with raw or cooked vegetables; one-quarter of it with whole grains; and one-quarter with lean protein, such as chicken, turkey, fish, beans, lentils, or tofu. (Again, look to Appendix B for options.) Make it a priority to cook with healthy fats and heart-healthy seasonings that are low in sodium.

Healthy Snacks

For most people, the words *healthy* and *snack* don't belong in the same sentence. That's because many of us snack on cookies, potato chips, cheese curls, and other highly processed foods that are rid-dled with sodium, fat, and calories. But snacking is an important part of a healthy eating plan, and most adults should have a mid-morning and a midafternoon snack each day. Healthy snacks keep energy levels up and control your appetite, making you less likely to overindulge at mealtime.

Healthy snacks don't always mean celery or raw broccoli, although those are very good choices. Just remember to factor

FIGURE 4.2 Balanced DASH Meal

your snacking into the rest of your overall eating plan. You can have a cookie every now and then, but try to make your snacks fruits, veggies, low-fat dips (hummus is an excellent choice), and nonsugary drinks. Include some protein along with some type of fruit, vegetable, or whole grain. The following are some healthy snack options:

- Carrots and hummus
- Whole-grain crackers and natural peanut butter
- Fruit and low-fat yogurt
- Trail mix made with whole-grain breakfast cereal, nuts, and dried fruit

ting the Most Benefit from
lits and Vegetables

No single type of fruit or vegetable can deliver all the benefits a broad range offers. Variety is the key. (The shopping list in Appendix C gives a variety of excellent choices.) Try to get at least one serving a day from each of the following categories:

- Dark green or leafy vegetables (dark lettuce, kale, spinach, broccoli)
- Yellow or orange fruits and vegetables (squash, carrots, nectarines, cantaloupe)
- Red fruits and vegetables (red peppers, tomatoes, strawberries)
- Legumes (lentils, chickpeas, kidney beans, black beans)
- Citrus fruits (oranges, grapefruits, lemons, limes)

Look for fruits and vegetables with strong colors—dark greens and deep oranges; some of their pigments (chemicals that provide color) are healthy phytochemicals.

Next Steps

Many of the healthy benefits that come from a well-planned diet (including weight loss, lower blood pressure, improved cholesterol levels, and protection from disease) can also be had—or enhanced—through a sensible exercise program. That's the topic of our next chapter. If you're ready to learn how you can walk, swim, dance, or cycle your blood pressure numbers down, let's begin.

CHAPTER 5

Exercise

Legend has it that Andrew Carnegie was once asked "Is it labor, capital, or intelligence that's most important in industry?" Carnegie responded with a question of his own: "Which is the most important leg of a three-legged stool?" His point is well taken; in order for the stool to balance, all three legs are equally important.

So far you've learned to develop two sturdy legs of the stool that will support your lifestyle modification approach to controlling your blood pressure: stress management and healthful eating. Now it's time to balance your program by adding exercise, the third leg. It's important to see each leg of your stool as existing in cooperation with, and support of, the other two. This may be especially important when it comes to exercise. Year after year the statistics confirm that we Americans just don't get up and move nearly as much as we ought to—namely, burning at least 1,000 to 1,400 calories a week in physical pursuits, or roughly thirty minutes of physical activity most days of the week. Close to one-third of adults get virtually no physical exercise at all. Coupled with our notoriously bad eating habits, this trend toward a sedentary lifestyle is a proven formula for deteriorating physical health. It's no coincidence that the most sedentary and overweight nation in the history of man also has the highest prevalence of heart disease.

Without exception, population studies of physical activity and health demonstrate that a sedentary lifestyle puts you at risk for chronic disease, including heart disease, diabetes, obesity, and certain types of cancer. In fact, the flip side is also true; regular physical activity is associated with many health benefits, including preventing and lowering high blood pressure.

Think of exercise not as a chore but as a gift you give yourself to stay healthy. In exchange for twenty-four hours of good health per day, every day, throughout your life, all your body asks in return is at least thirty minutes of moderate activity. We think it's plain to see who's getting the better end of *that* bargain. Just thirty minutes a day—and as we'll discuss later, they don't even have to be consecutive.

Let's get things started off right. Forget your visions of endless, boring sit-ups and push-ups. Forget your concerns about having to join a health club or buy expensive exercise equipment. Above all, get excited. Getting back on track with a physical activity regimen is guaranteed to be the most fun you'll ever have lowering your blood pressure—and the benefits don't stop there. Let's take a look at some of the many proven benefits of a physically active lifestyle.

How Exercise Helps People with Hypertension

According to Robert N. Butler at the National Institute on Aging, "If exercise could be put in a pill, it would be the most widely prescribed medicine in the world." The benefits of exercise go far beyond lowering your blood pressure, but because controlling your blood pressure is probably the main reason you're reading this book, we'll focus on how exercise can help you. Not only does regular exercise help prevent high blood pressure, but it's also a proven treatment for existing hypertension. The American College of Sports Medicine reviewed forty studies on the effect of exercise on blood pressure. With regular aerobic exercise, participants were able to reduce their systolic and diastolic pressures an average of 11 and 9 mm/Hg, respectively. Although many studies

The Gift of Exercise

The other day, I was looking for a gift to give a friend. This friend is very important to me and I want her to be around for a long time. I want her to live a long and healthy life. I thought how great it would be if I could give her a gift that would improve the quality of her life. So I sat down and made a list of what I would look for in this special gift:

- It would help her to be stronger, firmer, leaner, more flexible, and energetic.
- It would help lower her risk of dying from heart disease, help lower blood pressure and improve lipid profile, control glucose level, and fight obesity.
- It would help maintain balance and bone density, and help her age more gracefully.
- It would help improve immune system function, concentration, task performance, and quality of sleep.
- It would help reduce stress, improve mood, enhance self-esteem, and increase optimism and confidence.
- It would help increase self-awareness, spiritual well-being, and control over choices in her life.
- It would be fun but also challenging.
- It would allow for socialization but also for time alone, depending on her needs.
- It would come in all different modes and styles and could be adapted to various environments and weather conditions.
- Finally, it would have a good *Consumer Reports* rating, supported by scientific data from reputable sources.

After completing my list, I realized that the only gift that meets all my criteria is the gift of exercise. Have a healthy and happy life, my friend.

Jim Huddleston, M.S., P.T., Cardiac Wellness Program

focused on high-intensity exercises such as running, several evaluated the impact of more moderate activities such as walking. Surprisingly, moderate-intensity training provided the same, or even better, blood pressure–lowering benefits.

Need more reasons to get up and keep moving? In a study of severely hypertensive African American men, ten of the fourteen who rode a stationary bike for forty-five minutes three times a week were able to lower their dosage of antihypertensive medicine at the end of the thirty-two-week trial. In addition, echocardiograms showed that thickness of the heart wall had diminished in all the men who exercised. (A thickened heart wall raises your risk of stroke, abnormal heart rhythm, and heart attack.)

In 1995 a group of three studies found that, compared to the most physically active subjects, those who were the least active had a 30 percent greater chance of developing high blood pressure. A 1984 study in the *Journal of the American Medical Association* considered measures of cardiovascular fitness rather than just activity level. Following more than six thousand healthy people, ages twenty to sixty-five, over a twelve-year study period, the researchers determined that individuals who were the least fit had a 52 percent greater risk for substantially higher blood pressure. A review of fifty-four studies published in 2002 asserted that people who were less active and less fit had a 30–50 percent greater risk for high blood pressure. However, aerobic exercise was found to significantly reduce blood pressure in both overweight and normal-weight people.

Like any muscle, your heart grows stronger with exercise. A stronger heart pumps more blood more efficiently and with less force throughout your body. In addition to strengthening the heart muscle, here are some of the other ways that exercise helps improve your heart and the health of your vascular system.

 Prevents plaque buildup in arteries. Fatty deposits, called *plaques*, can build up on the artery walls to the point of restricting blood flow, a condition known as *atherosclerosis*, which may decrease adequate blood flow to the heart, brain, and vital organs (see Chapter 1). Exercise helps reduce these fatty deposits by increasing high-density lipoproteins (HDL) and decreasing triglycerides and low-density lipoproteins (LDL), when accompanied by weight loss. Every 1 mg/dL increase in HDL (e.g., increasing HDL from 39 to 40 mg/dL) lowers a person's risk of dying from heart disease by 2–3 percent.

 Protects arteries. Artery walls are lined with a thin layer of cells known as the *endothelium*, which produces a combination of chemicals that relax, contract, and lubricate the arteries to facilitate blood flow. As a result of high blood pressure, smoking, diabetes, high cholesterol, and the wear and tear of aging, the endothelium loses some of its natural ability to secrete these chemicals, which impairs the arteries' resilience and function. The good news is that recent advances in the study of vascular cell biology confirm that regular exercise can dramatically improve the functioning of the endothelium, even in people who already have atherosclerosis. Scientists believe that the regular expansion and contraction of arteries during exercise keeps the vessels "in shape" and helps maintain endothelial function.

Makes clots less likely. Besides narrowing arteries and impairing blood flow, plaque deposits jeopardize your heart health in another way. They can rupture, and when they do, your body dispatches specialized blood cells known as *platelets* to adhere to the site, resulting in a clot. The clot can sometimes partially or completely cut off blood flow to the heart. The latest scientific evidence reveals that regular exercise can inhibit clot formation by making the platelets less "sticky." It also promotes the release of enzymes that break down clots. Thus, in yet another way, it cuts your risk for heart disease and strokes.

The Benefits Just Keep on Coming

Yes, you should exercise to help control your blood pressure and improve the function of your heart and vascular system, but there are also other physical, mental, and emotional benefits. Here is a small sampling of what you'll have to look forward to when exercise becomes a regular part of your life.

- **Stronger bones.** Early in your life, your body builds bone faster than it loses it. But with age, bone is lost more rapidly than it's formed. Eventually, this leaves bones more fragile and susceptible to breaks. Exercise plays a key role in slowing bone loss. Exercises that involve bearing weight, such as running and jumping—and, to a lesser degree, walking—stress the skeleton and help keep it strong. But the best exercise for promoting bone strength is weight lifting (resistance training); when the muscles are challenged to lift weights, it also challenges the bones to which they are attached to become stronger.

- **Stronger immune system.** Regular moderate exercise increases your ability to fend off infection and, it appears, some forms of cancer. Experts believe this effect is due to a reduction in stress hormones and other chemicals that suppress immune activity during moderate exercise. Although the immune system returns to a pre-exercise state shortly after the exercise session is done, it appears that moderate activity on a daily or almost-daily basis has a cumulative benefit for your immune system, improving its ability to fight off infection.
- **Stronger muscles.** Strength training should not be reserved for young souls in search of buff bodies or bulked-up muscles. It is especially important to help maintain muscle mass and strength as we get older. Just about any activity becomes easier with stronger muscles. Weak muscles can make even minor exertion—walking a few blocks, climbing stairs, carrying groceries, or getting in and out of bed—difficult. Equally important, weak muscles compromise balance. Often a debilitating cycle is set in motion when a fall or disabling condition such as arthritis

curtails activity. It's natural to adapt to limitations, but many people find that the less they do, the less they are able to do as time goes on. People can maintain or regain (if limited by injury or inactivity) their strength and function with exercises that build muscle. People who exercise regularly and include strength training in their regimen stay functionally independent ten to twenty years longer than people who don't.

 • **Weight control.** A complete exercise program helps you control your weight in a couple of ways. When aerobic activity such as walking or swimming is sustained, you use stored body fat as the major fuel source to maintain the activity. The more physically active you are during the day, the more fat calories you burn and the fewer calories you store in your body. Exercise also helps to boost your metabolism, the calorie-burning furnace of your body. When you build new muscle, your body burns more calories throughout the day—even when you're sleeping—and that means that fewer calories will end up stored as fat. (It also may mean that you get to eat more—how's *that* for a benefit of exercise?) Both aerobic exercise and strength training are important for weight loss and long-term weight control.

 • **Improved mood.** Most people who exercise regularly will tell you that the exercise helps them feel better emotionally, as well as physically, and literature supports this observation. People across the emotional spectrum, from those with no depression to those with clinical depression, who get at least a moderate amount of exercise have fewer symptoms of depression. Exercise affects hormone production, including the level of hormones known as *endorphins*, the natural opiates that help block pain perception and may improve mood. (They are responsible for the sense of euphoria endurance athletes are said to experience, sometimes called a "runner's high.") Exercise also appears to increase the level of the brain chemical serotonin, which combats negative feelings.

Aside from releasing hormones, the improved strength, lost weight, and social opportunities afforded by exercise are a mood booster in themselves. People who exercise regularly feel good about themselves and enjoy improved self-esteem, self-awareness, and a sense of accomplishment.

- **Better mental functioning.** Hypertension is known to contribute to memory loss, so the fact that exercise can control hypertension means that it can help promote better memory. Regular physical activity also helps to keep mental processes sharp. The landmark MacArthur Foundation Study on aging revealed that people whose mental functions remained strong were active on a nearly daily basis. Recent studies found that cognitive decline was less prevalent in active older women, and walking was associated with a reduced risk of dementia in older men. The researchers offered several possible explanations for these cognitive function boosters. Exercise promotes improved blood flow to the brain, which may help maintain brain function and also directly stimulate the growth of neurons so connections between brain cells remain active.

A Note of Caution

No doubt about it, exercise is for everyone. But some exercises are not. You've heard it before, and you'll hear it again here: talk to your doctor before beginning a new exercise program. This is especially true for those with hypertension or heart disease. Light walking is probably safe for most people, but ask yourself these questions before you consider something more ambitious:

- Am I a man over forty-five or a woman over fifty-five who hasn't been physically active in the recent past?
- Have I ever had chest pain or pressure during or right after exercise?
- Have I experienced chest pain in the past month?

- Do I ever lose consciousness or fall over because of dizziness?
- Do I get breathless from even mild exertion?
- Has a doctor ever told me I have a heart condition?
- Have I ever suffered a heart attack or stroke?
- Has a doctor ever told me I can perform only medically supervised physical activity?
- Do I regularly take medicine for high blood pressure, stroke, or a heart condition?
- Has a doctor ever told me that I have muscle, joint, or bone problems that might be worsened by exercise?
- Do I take insulin or other medication for diabetes?
- Do I have another medical condition not mentioned here that might interfere with an exercise program?

If you answered yes to one or more of these questions, visit your doctor for a checkup. You may need more in-depth physical testing before starting your exercise program. If your heart disease is stable and your blood pressure is controlled, odds are good that many forms of exercise will be safe for you, provided you stay within your recommended guidelines. However, according to the American Heart Association and the American College of Sports Medicine, if you have a medical or musculoskeletal condition that is unstable or untreated, then exercise is not advised until your health status has stabilized.

Also, be aware that many drugs given to help treat heart disease or hypertension may affect you when you're exercising. Beta blockers, for example, keep your heart rate artificially low; that means your exercise heart rate (as measured against an industry standard for someone your age) is not a good indicator of how vigorously you are exercising. Vasodilators and angiotensin converting enzyme (ACE) inhibitors may make you more prone to dizziness from a drop in blood pressure if your postexercise cooldown is too short. Paying attention to how you feel physically (perceived exertion)—shortness of breath, level of fatigue, awareness of discomfort—is an important indicator of the intensity of your workout. Talk with your doctor or health care provider about the medications you take. If you work with an exercise professional, be sure he or she understands the potential effects.

Designing the Right Program for You

So you're primed and ready to get out there and walk, jog, cycle, or dance your way to lower blood pressure and slimmer-fitting jeans. That's great. But it's always good to walk before you run. Before you throw on your sneakers and hit the streets, you should take the time to understand the building blocks of a balanced exercise program.

Goals for regular physical activity and exercise can be divided into three categories: health benefit, fitness benefit, and performance benefit. We're not very concerned with striving for a performance benefit; that goal is usually reserved for the small percentage of people who want to achieve a personal best in a race or who need to perform at a high level for their job (professional/Olympic athletes). However, we are concerned about encouraging people to increase their physical activity for health and fitness.

Everything in Moderation

Today, exercise recommendations focus on moderate activity levels aimed at achieving functional fitness and avoiding disease. This differs from guidelines set out in the 1970s and 1980s, which emphasized high-intensity activity directed at achieving cardiovascular fitness. This shift took place for two reasons. First, subsequent research found that lower levels of activity offered substantial health benefits. Second, public health professionals believed that focusing on activity levels that are more manageable for the average person might help motivate an increasingly sedentary population.

A question that's often asked is, "How much do I have to do to improve my health?" As established in 1995 and still considered

Ways to Burn 150 Calories

- Washing and waxing a car for forty-five to sixty minutes
- Washing windows or floors for forty-five to sixty minutes
- Playing volleyball for forty-five minutes
- Playing touch football for thirty to forty-five minutes
- Gardening for thirty to forty-five minutes
- Wheeling self in wheelchair for thirty to forty minutes
- Walking one and a half miles in thirty minutes (twenty minutes/mile)
- Running one and a half miles in fifteen minutes (ten minutes/mile)
- Bicycling five miles in thirty minutes
- Dancing fast (social) for thirty minutes
- Pushing a stroller one and a half miles in thirty minutes
- Raking leaves for thirty minutes
- Performing water aerobics for thirty minutes
- Swimming laps for twenty minutes
- Playing wheelchair basketball for twenty minutes
- Playing basketball (shooting baskets) for thirty minutes
- Playing basketball (playing a game) for fifteen to twenty minutes
- Jumping rope for fifteen minutes
- Shoveling snow for fifteen minutes
- Climbing stairs for fifteen minutes

the standard today, the answer is, "at least thirty minutes of moderately intense physical activity, most or all days of the week." These thirty minutes can be accumulated throughout the day in segments as short as ten minutes. And just about everything counts: daily activities such as housecleaning, mowing the lawn, working in the garden, walking for errands; organized exercise such as using a treadmill or lifting weights; and playing games and sports. The benefit is really related to the number of calories burned while being active. Most adults burn about 150 to 200 calories in thirty minutes of moderate activity. If done most days of the week, this translates to 1,000 to 1,400 calories in a week, which is the level found to be effective for promoting overall health.

However, if weight loss is your goal, then thirty minutes is probably not enough. The new guidelines set forth by the Institutes of Medicine and U.S. Department of Agriculture encourage people who want to lose weight (and keep it off) to increase their physical exercise to sixty to ninety minutes per day, which will ensure a calorie burn of 300 to 500 calories per day.

Another popular way to measure how much activity you get during a day is to measure your steps with a pedometer. A pedometer is a gadget that you wear on your belt over your hip, and it counts the number of steps you take. Studies have shown that thirty minutes of moderate-intensity walking is equivalent to somewhere between 3,200 and 4,000 steps. Consequently, the goal for weight loss and maintenance of sixty to ninety minutes comes in at around 10,000 steps per day. In fact, a recent study in *Medicine and Science in Sports and Exercise* on the relationship between steps walked per day and body composition in middle-aged women found that the average body mass index of women who accumulated 10,000+ steps per day was in the normal range.

These recommendations were set up to encourage people to get up and move and spend less time in sedentary activities such as watching TV, surfing the Net, and driving cars. But if you really want to make a significant impact on your overall health—including building a strong, fit body—you may need to be a little more specific about the exercise you choose to do.

Three Components of a Good Exercise Program

A good exercise program for improving fitness has three components: aerobic activity, strength (resistance) training, and flexibility exercises. Each of these will benefit your body in a different way. Aerobic activity improves your heart health, lowers your risk for numerous diseases, and can lengthen your life span. Resistance exercises strengthen your muscles and bones and improve your body's ratio of lean muscle mass to fat. Flexibility training keeps your muscles stretched and your joints limber. But your exercise doesn't have to be strictly divided into specific categories. Variety and fun are what often keep exercise interesting. For example, you may want to take a yoga class for relaxation, practice t'ai chi to improve your balance, or schedule a weekly tennis or golf game to satisfy your need for friendly competition. Let's first take a look at those important three basic components.

 Aerobic Activity. Aerobic activity is also known as *cardiovascular exercise* and *endurance exercise*. It consists of repetitive motions involving contraction of the large muscle groups of the arms and legs, and it uses oxygen to help you burn fat as the major fuel source to power the activity. Most of the low-intensity activity you accumulate during your day falls into this category. At higher levels of exertion, aerobic exercise increases your breathing and heart rate and causes you to perspire. Aerobic exercise is the centerpiece of any fitness program. Nearly all of the research regarding the disease-fighting benefits of exercise revolves around cardiovascular activity, which includes walking, jogging, swimming, and cycling. The general recommendations for aerobic exercise are as follows: three to five times per week, thirty to sixty minutes at a time, at a moderate intensity (comfortable but challenging).

How can you tell when you are exercising at moderate intensity? One objective measure is to monitor your heart rate. The Karvonen formula helps you to determine your optimal exercise heart rate (EHR), which is shown as a percentage range of your maximum heart rate. Generally, exercising between 50 and 80 percent of your maximum capacity is considered a good, comfortable, challenging intensity. The Karvonen formula is as follows:

$$[(220 - \text{Age}) - \text{Resting heart rate}] \times \% \text{ of exercise intensity} + \text{Resting heart rate} = \text{EHR}$$

That may seem a little confusing, so let's look at an example step-by-step. Let's say you are forty years old and your resting heart rate (RHR) is 80 beats per minute, and you are aiming for 50–75 percent exercise intensity:

Step 1:   (220 − Age) − RHR
              (220 − 40) − 80 = 100

Step 2:   100 × % (the 50–75 percent you're aiming for)
              100 × 50% = 50; 100 × 75% = 75

Step 3:   Add RHR
              50 + 80 = 130; 75 + 80 = 155

Voilà! Your target EHR is between 130 and 155 beats per minute.

The other way to tell how hard you're working is to pay attention to your subjective experience of the exercise, or perceived exertion. How does the activity feel to you? You should feel a little short of breath but still able to carry on a conversation, and you should feel a little fatigued because you are challenging your body to work harder than usual. Don't be afraid to challenge yourself a little. That's how you'll grow stronger physically and spiritually. But you should not feel uncomfortably short of breath or overly fatigued, and you should not feel significant discomfort or pain. This is the "Goldilocks of exercise"—not too easy and not too hard, but just right.

Recent research has shown that you can get some good cardiovascular benefits even if you break your thirty-minute total into three ten-minute stints, provided they're of equal intensity compared to a longer thirty-minute bout. Although there are conditioning benefits associated with interval training (alternating higher- and lower-intensity bouts within your target heart rate zone), you should avoid infrequent bouts of very high-intensity activity. This is not the best approach to exercise for general health and fitness and is not recommended for several reasons. First, reducing your risk for hypertension, high cholesterol, type 2 diabetes, and other conditions depends on the total volume of your exercise rather than its intensity. Second, higher-intensity activity raises your chances for muscle or joint injury and for sudden death as a result of heart rhythm disturbances. Third, very high-intensity exercise can be quite uncomfortable and requires a lot of motivation, both of which are triggers for poor compliance.

Strength Training. Although aerobic activity is most commonly cited as the key to cardiovascular health, studies show that strength training, such as weight lifting, is also associated with many health benefits. In the past, doctors cautioned people with heart disease or hypertension against strength training out of fear that the abrupt surges of blood pressure that can accompany such exercises might be dangerous. But new recommendations from the American Heart Association suggest that moderate (comfortable) resistance training can be safe and beneficial for most patients with hypertension and heart disease.

Strength training is important for building muscle and bone. Without strength training, a thirty-year-old individual can expect to lose 25 percent of muscle mass by age seventy and another 25 percent by age ninety. The good news is that a person who begins strength training can increase strength by 30–100 percent over a period of months. Technically speaking, strength training occurs any time a contracting muscle is faced with a stronger-than-usual counterforce, such as doing elastic-band workouts and using weight machines or free weights. The general recommendations for strength training are as follows: one to two sets of eight to twelve repetitions for each exercise, two to three nonconsecutive days per week. The amount of weight lifted should produce muscle fatigue (without struggling or straining) at the completion of repetitions.

Flexibility Exercises. The third component of a balanced exercise program is stretching. Muscles tend to shorten and weaken with age. Shorter, stiffer muscle fibers make you vulnerable to injuries, pain, and stress. Moreover, the lubricating secretions that kept muscles moving efficiently in your youth dry up as the years go by. But regularly performing exercises that isolate and stretch your muscles and tendons can counteract this process. In addition, the increased blood flow to the muscles that accompanies exercise helps them become more limber. Stretching also improves your posture and balance because well-stretched muscles move more easily through their entire range of motion, resulting in better function and performance.

Recent studies have shown that in most cases it doesn't matter when you stretch as long as you spend time stretching. The old belief that it was necessary to stretch before exercise to reduce the risk of injury proved not to be true. However, if you know you carry muscle tension in a particular body part that will be stressed during exercise, you might want to do some slow, mindful stretching before you begin more vigorous activity. Stretching after exercise is often recommended, as muscles do tend to tighten up with use, and cooldown is a great time to pay attention to how you are feeling physically, emotionally, and spiritually. The general recommendations for stretching and flexibility are as follows: stretch two to three days per week; hold each stretch for ten to twenty seconds and repeat three to five times; stretch to mild discomfort, not to pain. Doing a series of yoga stretches such as the Sun Salutation (Surya Namaskar; traditionally performed in the early morning while facing the sun) seen in Figure 5.1 is a wonderful way to stretch and bring variety and a quality of mindfulness and relaxation into your exercise practice. This and other yoga stretches are an effective way to develop and maintain musculoskeletal health by releasing muscle tension, increasing flexibility, improving posture, facilitating breath control, and cultivating mind-body awareness.

You can get all three components—aerobic, strength, and flexibility—from any number of physical activities you may already

FIGURE 5.1 Sun Salutation Stretch

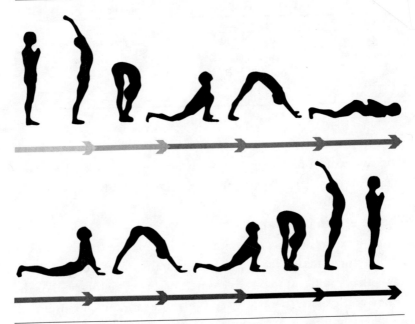

Move in and out of each posture slowly and cautiously as you become familiar with it, learning the correct body mechanics and proper sequence. Listen to your body, and resist the temptation to push yourself or strain. Once you are comfortable with the entire sequence, you may synchronize your body movements with the rhythm of your breathing: inhaling when the upper body stretches or expands, exhaling when bending over. While you may not have the degree of flexibility shown here, you will gradually increase your flexibility. For more specific information on performing the Sun Salutation, see the Yoga Journal website at yogajournal.com/practice/1040_1.cfm. Adapted image courtesy of Santosha.com.

enjoy. That's important to know. If you don't enjoy your exercise program, you are far more likely to find excuses to put it off. The best activity (or combination of activities) for you to do is the one you'll enjoy because you will be more willing to keep doing it. It would be great if everyone could include all the recommendations in Table 5.1 in their exercise routine, but history tells us that it is not going to happen. Nor is it realistic. But making sure that the environment, the setting, and the activity itself are enjoyable will

TABLE 5.1 Your Exercise Prescription

Exercise Type	Duration	Frequency
Warm-up	5–10 minutes	Whenever you exercise
Aerobics	20–60 minutes	3–5 times/week
Muscle toning	15–30 minutes 1–2 sets of 8–12 repetitions	2–3 times/week
Cooldown	5–10 minutes	Whenever you exercise

work wonders for keeping you motivated and committed to making exercise an integral part of your total program for good health.

The Exercise Continuum

Think of exercise as a continuum. At one end are the activities of daily living—raking leaves, taking the stairs instead of the elevator—that you fit into your day as part of an active lifestyle. At the other end of the spectrum are the more organized, sustained, moderately intense activities that make up a structured exercise program. This is where you reap the maximum rewards. Somewhere along the spectrum lie the sports and recreational activities you do for pleasure and relaxation. So take a look at where you see yourself starting along the spectrum, and begin to reap some of those health benefits we told you about.

Getting Started: What Works for You?

Maybe you already have an idea in mind for what kind of exercises you would like to do. Then again, maybe you would like to try some things you've never tried before. That can be a good idea and a great way to keep things fresh and interesting. It might also be a great way to make new friends if you happen to join a walking group or take a yoga class.

There is no right or wrong here—unless, of course, what you've chosen to do could be harmful. It should come as no surprise that the most successful exercise program is one that's well suited to the individual. To give yourself the best odds of sticking

Tips for Exercising Safely

These pointers are good advice for everyone who exercises, regardless of age, conditioning, or intensity of exercise:

- Warm up and cool down properly. (See "Mind-Body Exercises as Warm-Ups and Cooldowns" later in the chapter.)
- If you have a cold, it's okay to exercise, but monitor how you feel and adjust your efforts accordingly; exercising too vigorously may lower your immune response.
- Wait at least two hours after eating a full meal to exercise.
- In hot, humid weather, watch for signs of overheating, which include headache, dizziness, nausea, fainting, cramps, or palpitations.
- Slow down when going up hills.
- Dress in loose, comfortable clothing that's appropriate for the weather. Wear layers in cold weather—an inner layer of lightweight synthetic fabric, a middle layer for insulation if necessary, and a loose-fitting outer layer to protect against the elements—and light, synthetic blends in warm weather to help wick moisture away from your skin.
- Choose shoes that are designed for your type of exercise and replace them regularly.
- Don't overexert. Listen to your body and cut back if you need to. Remember to keep it comfortable but challenging.
- Always remember to drink plenty of water before, during, and after exercise. If you lose weight during exercise, you are not drinking enough.
- If you experience any of the following symptoms while exercising, stop your activity and see a doctor promptly:

  Aching, burning, tightness, or a feeling of fullness in the upper body

  Faintness or loss of consciousness

  Shortness of breath that takes more than five minutes to go away or wheezing

  Pain in bones or joints

with a program, stack the deck in your favor by asking yourself a few questions to help you think carefully about the form of exercise that's right for you:

- **What kind of setting works for you?** Do you have easy access to a pool? If not, swimming probably isn't a good choice. Likewise, if you live in a particularly hot or cold climate, certain outdoor activities may not be sustainable. On the other hand, if there's a network of biking and jogging trails near your office, a routine of lunchtime excursions might be just the ticket.

- **Do you like exercising alone or with others?** Many people find the solitude of swimming or running ideal for contemplation. Others enjoy the motivation and support of a group aerobics class or a walking companion.

- **How much money do you want to spend?** You'll need to weigh expense against other factors, such as the ability to exercise indoors or to participate in a particular activity. Many exercise options are available at a range of prices. You can get great workouts for virtually no money by walking, running, or hiking. A set of inexpensive home barbells or Therabands (resistance bands) can produce similar strength results as using weight machines at a health club. However, some people may find that the money they spend for gym privileges is a motivating factor. Only you know what will work best in your particular case.

- **What's your current level of fitness?** If you've been sedentary for a while, it's unrealistic (not to mention dangerous) to attempt a five-mile run your first day out. One of the quickest ways to sabotage an exercise program is with an injury. A more practical approach would be to start with short walks and work up to greater levels of intensity and duration as your level of fitness increases. If you've had previous injuries or suffer from a chronic disease, talk to your doctor about your physical limitations before deciding on a type of exercise.

- **What are your exercise goals?** Although ideally everyone's workout would include aerobic, strengthening, and flexibility components, that is not always practical. Depending on your own activity and health goals, you may want to focus on a particular area. For example, a weight-loss program would require a greater emphasis on calorie-burning aerobic activities. If flexibility and balance are your main concerns, you may want to spend more time practicing t'ai chi or yoga.

Exercise: Great for Mind and Body

We've discussed how exercise is great for your body and great for your mind. But it's also great for the body *and* mind. What does that mean? By involving the mind to monitor the body's movements and sensations, and by allowing those movements and sensations to promote a sharp mental focus, you've tuned in to the feedback loop that is at the heart of the mind-body connection. When body and mind work seamlessly together, you may describe yourself as feeling "on" or "in the moment." You lose track of time. You feel focused and alert, and at the same time, you're profoundly calm and relaxed. Your mind is quiet on the inside, while your body is physically active on the outside. This kind of relaxation doesn't come with one particular type of activity. The rhythmic movements and deep breathing involved in aerobic exercises, such as walking, running, and swimming, provide opportunities for contemplation and relaxation. Stretching, too, releases muscle tension and promotes a feeling of calm while providing a focus for the mind in monitoring how the body really feels as it stretches. Even weight lifting can be done with a focused awareness as the weights are lifted and lowered in time to the breath, and the mind pays attention to how the muscles respond to the challenge. However, certain disciplines such as yoga, t'ai chi, and Pilates inherently combine tension-releasing physical movement with an emphasis on mental focus and meditation. For practitioners, the results—apart from improved strength, flexibility, and balance—can be stress reduction, pain relief, and a general sense of well-being. Let's take a closer look at these mind-body exercises.

Yoga

This style of movement had its genesis as a spiritual practice in ancient India. There are several styles of yoga. Hatha yoga, the form commonly practiced in the West, combines focused breathing (*pranayama*) with movement in and out of body postures (*asanas*). The movements consist of forward and backward bends, twists, and inversions, as well as standing and balancing poses. Practicing yoga can release tension and stiffness, improve balance, and help you achieve inner peace, calm, and spiritual awareness. Other benefits include increased strength, vitality, and coordination. Weight-bearing yoga poses can also promote bone health. In particular, inverted poses that involve bearing weight in the upper extremities can stimulate bones in the hands, arms, and torso. Some kinds of yoga, such as Ashtanga yoga (or its westernized version, power yoga) and Bikram yoga, are particularly intense and provide a more challenging physical workout.

T'ai Chi

Developed in China more than seven hundred years ago from the martial arts tradition, t'ai chi evolved out of the Taoist principle that the balanced life force, called *chi* (or Qi), is responsible for good health as it flows throughout the body. The discipline incorporates a series of slow, graceful movements that look like an effortless, slow-motion dance and require unbroken concentration to execute. The goal is to invigorate the practitioner's chi, integrating mind and body, by keeping the muscles active but relaxed and the mind alert but calm. Because t'ai chi builds strength and flexibility, it can improve posture and balance. A 1996 study in the *Journal of the American Geriatric Society* reported a nearly 50 percent reduction in falls among elderly people who participated in a fifteen-week program of t'ai chi. Studies also suggest that programs lasting four to twelve months help to lower blood pressure and improve conditioning of the heart and lungs.

Pilates

This rigorous discipline was developed by Joseph Pilates, a German boxer and fitness trainer, who brought his technique to the United States in the 1920s. Pilates consists of a series of exercises designed to strengthen, lengthen, and tone the body and can be performed using specially designed pieces of equipment or as floor exercises. At the core of the Pilates method is a philosophy of focus and concentration founded on yoga and Zen meditation. The Pilates system relies on gravity to enable the body to supply its own resistance to strengthen core muscle groups. It emphasizes deep, coordinated breathing; concentration; precision and control; and visualized movements to encourage physical, emotional, and spiritual strengthening.

Mind-Body Exercises as Warm-Ups and Cooldowns

You wouldn't bake a cake without preheating the oven. Preheating is essential for even cooking, keeping the baking within its recommended time frame and improving the quality of the finished product. The same goes for your body when it comes to exercise. Preheating—or warming up—increases blood flow, respiration, and body temperature, helping to warm and stretch the muscles, which may protect them from injury. It also warms and thins the fluids that protect your joints, making the joints move more smoothly and with less effort. Slowly increasing the intensity of aerobic exercise over five to ten minutes is a good way to warm up. In addition, the great thing about some elements of yoga, t'ai chi, and Pilates is that, when modified properly, they make great warm-ups.

Going back to our cake analogy, you wouldn't eat a cake fresh from the oven before it's had a chance to cool down. Again, the same goes for you. Cooling down prevents a rapid drop in heart rate and blood pressure, and it also prevents blood from pooling in the extremities. Gradually decreasing the intensity of aerobic exercise facilitates the cooldown process, and simple stretching or yoga postures, or fluid movements as in t'ai chi, are superb options for transitioning into and out of more vigorous exercise. The mindful nature of these activities provides an opportunity to increase awareness of how your body feels so that you can make healthy decisions about how you choose to exercise on a day-to-day basis.

Carol's Story

When we met Carol back in Chapter 2, we learned that regular exercise was a challenge for her. She began a walking program but stayed with it only because she made it a priority and because she knew intellectually that it would help lower her blood pressure. However, as she became more comfortable with her relaxation response practice, she became more aware of what she needed and how she felt. She realized that she enjoyed taking care of herself and that she felt much better physically and emotionally when she exercised. She began to appreciate that, combined with stress management, exercise helped her to feel calmer and able to handle the challenges of the day with greater clarity and efficiency.

In taking the time to appreciate her relationship with exercise, Carol developed a sense of what worked for her and what didn't. She had to exercise first thing in the morning, or she probably wouldn't do it. If she walked alone, books on tape helped motivate her, but she also enjoyed walking with a friend. She did better with a destination, rather than just walking for the sake of walking—in doing so she began to incorporate walking into many of her daily activities, such as walking to the store or library and doing errands with her son. The more exercise she added into her life, the better she felt about herself physically, emotionally, and spiritually. She now feels secure enough about the importance of exercise in her life that when things get really busy and time is short, she can cut back on her exercise to meet other demands, knowing that the next day or the next week she will resume her usual routine. This has allowed her to build up to six to eight hours of exercise almost every week, a good amount to help control her blood pressure and to help her lose weight. It has become part of her self-identity and who she is.

Staying in It for the Long Haul

Exercise isn't something you do just until your blood pressure numbers start to look better or when you want to drop a couple of extra pounds here and there. To be successful, it has to be thoroughly integrated into your lifestyle; it should be something you do as routinely as eating, sleeping, and taking your morning shower. Unfortunately, as you may know from firsthand experience, this is easier said than done. Statistics show that more health club memberships are sold in early January (New Year's resolution time) than any month of the year. But come February or March, more than half of those new members have quit. Similarly, in a moment of inspiration and great resolve, you may have purchased a piece of exercise equipment, only to let it gather dust in a corner of your basement.

Keeping your eye on the prize will help you stick to the program. You know that a balanced exercise program will make you stronger and slimmer and may help you lower or control your blood pressure. But knowing the intrinsic benefits of lifelong exercise or even creating a personal exercise plan isn't enough. As you begin your exercise program, you'll need a solid dose of motivation and preparation to keep you on track and overcome the challenges that you'll inevitably come across.

Set Some Goals. Making an overnight change from a sedentary lifestyle to regular exercise isn't in the cards for most people. What's more, unrealistic expectations will set you up for frustration and failure. A better approach is first to set a long-term goal for the coming year. Since this goal can be daunting when you think about it as a whole, break it into weekly or monthly targets. Although your goal may be to lose twenty-five pounds in a year, you may want to focus instead on losing just over two pounds a month. Because it takes a deficit of about 3,500 calories to lose a pound, you would need to walk about seventy miles a month (one mile burns roughly 100 calories) or seventeen and a half miles a week. Walking briskly at three to four miles per hour, you can accomplish that goal with six or seven 45-minute walks each week. This is, of course, provided you don't make any changes in your diet or cut back on the amount of other physical activity you get. By making dietary changes, including decreasing caloric intake, you could exercise even less and still lose weight.

Reward Your Efforts. Motivation can be divided into two categories: intrinsic and extrinsic. When something is intrinsically motivating, the pleasure that comes from doing the activity itself is all the push you need to go ahead and do it. But sometimes you need a little extra push. This is what extrinsic motivation is all about: it's the motivation to do an activity based on the anticipated pleasure of some outside reward. There will be times when that nice, warm bed seems a heck of a lot nicer than the treadmill in the basement. This is when an extrinsic reward will give you the push you need. Maybe you'll promise yourself to indulge in a professional massage if you stick with the program throughout the month, or that you'll go to see a movie at the end of the week. Just be sure to give yourself those rewards only after you've met the goal you've set. Studies show that people who have been successful at maintaining a long-term exercise program did well initially by making it a priority. But what kept them going were positive feelings that accrued from being active: pep and energy, enjoyment, better sleep, and feeling more alert and relaxed.

Chart Your Progress. Once you've set your goal, you can begin to measure your performance. Record your minutes walked each day in a daily planner or make a simple chart that you can post on the refrigerator. Either way, keep a written record of what you have accomplished. You can create similar charts for your strength training and stretching programs.

Celebrate Your Victories. Meeting your exercise goals, even short-term ones, is cause for celebration. It reflects your commitment to improving your health. Find ways to pat yourself on the back. Whether your reward is small or large, make sure it's something meaningful and enjoyable. Rewards to avoid are those things that you may regret soon after, such as eating an ice cream cone if your ultimate goal is losing weight. A better choice might be a new CD to listen to while you walk.

Call for Backup. If you happen to prefer exercising with a partner or in a group, the peer support can be a tremendous boost for those days when you'd sooner stay in bed under the covers than lace up your sneakers and get moving. But even if you don't prefer exercising with others, you can still benefit from a little support every now and then. Tell your spouse, children, friends, family, and coworkers about your goal, and ask them to give you encouragement—and pressure, if necessary—to stick to it.

Make It Fit. For most people, time constraints are a major problem to overcome. Start planning your exercise sessions by making a detailed schedule of your week. Look for ways you can work in blocks of exercise. Can you get up half an hour earlier every morning for a walk? Would this mean going to bed earlier? Be realistic. Don't schedule exercise for after dinner if you know that's when you always help the kids with their homework. In addition to the time you schedule, look for ways to add bits of activity and recreational exercise every day: take an extra lap around the mall when you're shopping or a Saturday morning bike ride; take the stairs instead of the elevator or escalator whenever possible; mow your own lawn; during your coffee or lunch break, go for a walk, clear your head, and recharge your battery.

After the first week, adjust your schedule in places where it may not be working. The good news is that as your conditioning increases, you'll be able to boost the intensity of your exercise without exerting yourself further. This means that you'll be able to fit more into your allotted time—for example, walking four miles in the time it used to take you to do three.

Turn Off That Negative Thinking. Remember that you learned in Chapter 3 to notice negative thinking. If negative thoughts about exercise are getting in your way, tell yourself to stop, take a breath, and reflect on what is behind those thoughts. What perceptions and beliefs about yourself—and exercise in general—influence your choice not to exercise? Then try to reframe to more positive thoughts to help you get back on track. (Remember: jumping to conclusions doesn't count as exercise!)

Getting Back on Track

Even the most dedicated exercisers sometimes go astray. Almost anything can knock you off track: a bad cold, an out-of-town trip, or a stretch of bad weather. A setback does not mean that you've failed; it just means that you need to start again—immediately. That's why it's critical to learn how to reclaim your routine. When you've missed workout sessions, you need to evaluate your current level of fitness and set goals accordingly. If you've been away from your routine for two weeks or more, don't expect to start where you left off. Cut back on your workout the first few days and then gradually increase your effort as your body readjusts to the challenge.

The bigger challenge may come in getting yourself back in an exercising frame of mind. Try to keep confidence in yourself when you relapse. Instead of expending energy on feeling guilty and defeated, focus on what it'll take to get started again. Once you resume your program, you'll be amazed at how quickly it will begin to feel natural. Here are a few tricks you might try to rekindle your motivation:

- Imagine yourself exercising. Recall the aspects of exercise you enjoy most.
- Come up with a tantalizing reward to give yourself when you meet your first goal after resuming your program.
- Line up walking or jogging partners for your next few outings.
- If completing your whole exercise routine seems overwhelming, mentally divide it into smaller chunks and give yourself the option of stopping at the end of each one. However, when you reach a checkpoint, encourage yourself to move on to the next one instead of quitting.
- Rather than focusing on why you don't want to exercise, concentrate on how good you feel when you've finished a workout.

Next Steps

Where do we go from here? Throughout this book, our goal is clear and simple: to educate you about hypertension and give you the tools to manage it through lifestyle modification. Stress management, healthy diet, and sensible exercise will set you well on your way to reclaiming your physical and emotional health.

Occasionally, you may need medication in addition to self-care techniques to optimally manage your blood pressure. We will discuss blood pressure medication in the next chapter.

CHAPTER 6

When Is Medication Necessary?

If you've been diagnosed with hypertension, the question of whether you need to be on medication will almost inevitably come up. While our goal throughout this book has been to give you natural tools to lower blood pressure, sometimes your doctor will determine that medication is necessary. Don't consider it an either/or situation. Medication and lifestyle modification work well together, and the mind-body program presented in this book has helped many people reduce or eliminate their need for medication. We must stress, however, that you should make changes to your prescribed medication only under a doctor's supervision. In this chapter, we'll discuss why medication may be necessary and the various types of blood pressure medication available.

Why You May Need Medication

Several large studies show that the chances of heart attack, stroke, heart failure, chronic kidney disease, and premature death start creeping up at the very common blood pressure of 115/75 mm/Hg. From there on, every twenty-point increase in systolic pressure (the top number) or ten-point increase in diastolic pressure (the bottom number) doubles the risk of health problems.

You may remember from our explanation in Chapter 1 that the body's mechanisms for controlling blood pressure are vast and complex. Given these many mechanisms, there are a number of ways something could go wrong. Blood vessels can become stiffer and less elastic as we age, as well as less responsive to the chemical messengers that regulate blood pressure.

Hypertension and Congestive Heart Failure

If your blood pressure is not well controlled, you are twice as likely to suffer heart failure than is someone with normal blood pressure. Hypertension forces the heart to work harder to pump blood throughout the body. As a result, the left ventricle, the heart's main pumping chamber, becomes thicker and more muscular in order to contract with greater force. This compensation, known as *left ventricular hypertrophy* (LVH), eventually becomes counterproductive. Unlike your biceps, the thickness of your heart muscle doesn't translate into strength. As the heart muscle enlarges, it needs more and more oxygen, but the arteries, which also thicken and narrow as a result of hypertension, become less able to deliver it.

The combination of LVH and damaged arteries may eventually render your heart unable to pump blood efficiently. Without an adequate supply of blood, your heart weakens, and this in turn can lead to a condition known as *congestive heart failure*.

Hypertension and Stroke

Untreated hypertension is the leading cause of stroke. Two-thirds of people having a first stroke have blood pressures higher than 160/95 mm/Hg. Each year, over half a million people in the United States have their first stroke (an average of one person every forty-five seconds) and nearly 167,000 will die from stroke. That makes it the third leading cause of death in the country, following heart disease and cancer, and it is also the number-one cause of long-term disability.

A stroke is a medical emergency that is every bit as dire as a heart attack, a similarity that has led experts to call it a "brain attack." Just as a heart attack reduces the blood supply to an area of the heart, a stroke reduces blood supply to an area of the brain. Deprived of blood, some of the brain cells die, possibly taking with them the ability to move, speak, feel, think, or even recognize people.

Hypertension and Dementia

By encouraging atherosclerosis, hypertension can contribute to memory loss and dementia. Atherosclerosis interferes with circulation, and a lack of blood can produce areas of dead tissue in the brain called *small infarcts*. Multi-infarct dementia, a well-recognized cause of memory loss in older people, is caused by a series of tiny strokes. Each one affects such a small area of the brain that symptoms may not be apparent until a substantial amount of tissue has been destroyed.

Hypertension and Kidney Disease

The kidneys play a critical role in the body's control of blood pressure by regulating the amount of water and sodium in circulation. When blood pressure rises, the kidneys excrete water and sodium. This action helps bring the pressure back down by stimulating the loss of body fluids (through urination, for example), thereby reducing the volume of circulating blood. When blood pressure falls, the kidneys retain water and sodium to conserve blood volume and raise pressure.

Sustained high blood pressure damages the structures in the kidneys, called *glomeruli*, that filter waste products, sodium, and water from the bloodstream; this results in kidney failure. Uncontrolled hypertension is second only to diabetes as a cause of end-stage renal disease (which may require dialysis or kidney transplantation) and accounts for about 26 percent of new cases.

Classes of Hypertensive Medication

Several classes of medication are currently used. Each has its own function, along with its own unique benefits and potential side effects.

Diuretics

Commonly called *water pills*, diuretics are the oldest and least expensive class of medications used to treat hypertension. They help the kidneys eliminate sodium and water from the body. This process decreases blood volume, so your heart has less to pump with each beat, which in turn lowers blood pressure. Diuretics are especially effective for salt-sensitive patients with hypertension and older patients with isolated systolic hypertension.

The Joint National Committee on Prevention, Detection, Evaluation, and Treatment of High Blood Pressure (JNC 7) recommends that thiazide be the initial medication used for most people diagnosed with hypertension and suggests that they be part of treatment for most individuals taking multiple medications to control their blood pressure. Thiazide diuretics act on the kidney to stop sodium from reentering circulation.

Common side effects of these drugs include frequent urination, light-headedness, fatigue, and muscle cramps. Diuretics can cause gout, a painful form of arthritis caused by the buildup of uric acid in the body, because they elevate blood levels of this substance. Some common thiazide diuretics include Diuril and Hydrodiuril. A common loop diuretic, which acts on another part of the kidney, is Lasix.

Peripheral Adrenergic Receptor Blockers

These medications work by preventing neurotransmitters from attaching to cells and stimulating the heart and blood vessels. They are divided into two major groups: beta blockers and alpha blockers.

Beta blockers, which have been used since the 1960s, lock on to cell structures called *beta receptors*, the same receptors that certain neurotransmitters (primarily epinephrine) normally attach themselves to in order to stimulate the heart. By preventing the neurotransmitters from activating heart cells, beta blockers cause the heart rate to slow and blood pressure to fall. Beta blockers come in two varieties—cardioselective and nonselective. Either type can worsen asthma or other chronic lung disorders, but the nonselective agents are potentially more dangerous for people with respiratory problems. They can also worsen the risk of heart failure in some patients, while improving it in others. They can mask the warning signs of hypoglycemia (low blood sugar) in patients with diabetes.

The most common side effects of beta blockers are fatigue, depression, erectile dysfunction, shortness of breath, insomnia, and reduced tolerance for exercise. Some common beta blockers include Tenormin, Lopressor, Nadolol, Inderal, Timolol, and Zebeta.

Alpha blockers are similar in action to beta blockers, but they work on the sites where neurotransmitters that cause vessel constriction (primarily norepinephrine) attach themselves. Drugs called *alpha-1 blockers* impede alpha receptors in the heart and blood vessels. They may be especially useful for hypertensive patients with high cholesterol. In addition to reducing blood pressure, alpha-1 blockers also reduce "bad" low-density lipoprotein (LDL) cholesterol levels and increase "good" high-density lipoprotein (HDL) cholesterol. These medications may improve insulin sensitivity in patients with glucose intolerance and hyperglycemia (high blood sugar). They are also prescribed for men with benign prostatic hyperplasia, a noncancerous enlargement of the prostate gland, because they relax smooth muscles surrounding the prostate, relieving the constriction of the urethra and easing urine flow.

Side effects of alpha blockers include orthostatic hypotension (a rise in blood pressure on standing up), heart palpitations, dizziness, nasal congestion, headaches, and dry mouth. They can also cause erectile dysfunction, although not as frequently as some other blood pressure medications. Some common ones include Cardura, Minipress, and Hytrin.

Some patients require both alpha and beta blockers to control their blood pressure. The drugs Normodyne and Coreg have properties of both.

Direct-Acting Vasodilators

Direct-acting vasodilators relax the arterial blood vessels. They act quickly and are often used in hypertensive emergencies. However, they can cause fluid retention and tachycardia (fast heart rate), so doctors usually prescribe them in combination with another blood pressure medication that slows heart rate, such as a cardioselective beta blocker. Apresoline and Loniten, the direct-acting vasodilators most commonly used to treat hypertension, can cause headaches, weakness, flushing, and nausea. In addition, Loniten can cause hair growth, fluid retention, and hyperglycemia.

Calcium-Channel Blockers

Calcium-channel blockers (CCBs) slow the movement of calcium into the smooth-muscle cells of the heart and blood vessels. This reduces the strength of heart muscle contractions and increases dilation of blood vessels, lowering blood pressure. Because calcium-channel blockers also slow nerve impulses in the heart, they are often prescribed for arrhythmia (irregular heartbeat). Common side effects of CCBs are headache, edema (water retention), heartburn, bradycardia (slow heart rate), and constipation. Common CCBs include Cardizem, Cartia, Norvasc, Plendil, and Procardia.

Angiotension-Converting Enzyme Inhibitors

This class of drugs, introduced in 1981, has proved widely effective in treating hypertension. These agents prevent your kidneys from retaining sodium and water by deactivating angiotensin-converting enzyme (ACE), which converts inactive angiotensin I to active angiotensin II. Angiotensin II raises blood pressure by triggering sodium and water retention and constricting the arteries. ACE inhibitors reduce blood pressure in most patients and produce fewer side effects than many other antihypertensive drugs. In addition, ACE inhibitors protect the kidneys of people with diabetes and kidney dysfunction and the hearts of people with congestive heart failure.

The most common side effects of these drugs are a reduced sense of taste and a dry cough. They can also cause potassium retention; therefore, people with poor kidney function must use them cautiously. Common ACE inhibitors include Lotensin, Captopril, Vasotec, Zestril, and Accupril.

Receptor Blockers: Fooling the Body

The discovery of the "lock-and-key" system of cell communication opened the door to a new world of drug research. The search began with a simple question: Why do some cells react to particular chemicals but not to others? The answer is both maddeningly complex and blessedly simple.

Chemicals circulating through the blood, such as hormones and neurotransmitters, stimulate cells. At any given moment, a cell may come in contact with hundreds of different chemicals, so it must be selective about which ones it responds to. To do this, cells have special structures, called *receptors*, on their outer surfaces. A receptor operates much like a car's ignition switch. Only a chemical with the right molecular configuration (the key) will fit the receptor (the lock) and start up biological activity inside the cell.

Researchers have used their knowledge of this system to formulate drugs that prevent cells from responding to certain substances. Beta blockers, which are used to treat hypertension, are a prime example. At times of stress and during exercise, your nerve cells release the neurotransmitters epinephrine and norepinephrine. When epinephrine attaches to beta receptors on heart cells, the cells are activated, increasing your heart rate and the strength of your heart's contractions. This raises your blood pressure. But beta blockers attach to the same receptors, because their structure has been carefully designed to fit neatly into the same "lock." With this spot filled, epinephrine and norepinephrine are unable to connect to the receptor, thus breaking the chain of chemical communication that would otherwise stimulate the heart and spark an increase in blood pressure.

Angiotensin II Receptor Blockers

This class of medication, approved for treating hypertension since 1995, blocks angiotensin II from constricting the blood vessels and stimulating salt and water retention. Because angiotensin receptor blockers (ARBs) are highly effective and well tolerated by most people, they have become quite popular. They don't produce any of the traditional side effects of other antihypertensive medications, and they're less likely to cause a cough as ACE inhibitors do. In addition, like ACE inhibitors, they benefit patients with diabetes, congestive heart failure, or both. Common ARBs include Avapro, Cozaar, Benicar, and Diovan.

Choosing the Right Medication

As we mentioned earlier, if you can't control your blood pressure through lifestyle changes and you are in good general health, the JNC 7 recommends trying thiazide diuretics first.

Doctors can choose from an abundant selection of antihypertensive medication, including many preparations that combine two or more drugs. Many newer antihypertensive drugs have a slightly different chemical structure from older drugs but produce nearly identical effects in the body. Others act in entirely different ways. Physicians can tailor treatment to the individual patient and can often prescribe medication that controls blood pressure, produces few or no side effects, and (we hope) protects against complications. Most important, it's often possible to use a single medication to treat both the hypertension and accompanying medical problems, such as congestive heart failure.

The JNC 7 recommends starting any antihypertensive drug at the lowest possible dose and gradually increasing it until the desired goal is reached. If the drug doesn't lower pressure or if it causes troublesome side effects, it should be replaced with a different one.

The usual course of treatment for stage 1 hypertension is to begin with one drug and add a second if your blood pressure does not decrease to desired levels (usually less than 140/90 mm/Hg, less than 130/80 mm/Hg for those with diabetes or chronic kidney disease). The treatment for stage 2 hypertension often begins with a two-drug combination. A third may be added if your blood pressure doesn't drop to an acceptable level. With all stages of hypertension and even prehypertension, lifestyle changes are an essential component of treatment.

A number of factors, including age and other health problems, will influence your doctor's decision about medication. The following are a few of the parameters he or she will use:

- **Older people.** For the elderly, the JNC 7 recommends thiazide diuretics, either alone or in combination with beta blockers, but calcium-channel blockers are often used also. Older people should not use medications that are prone to cause orthostatic hypotension (a sudden drop in blood pressure upon standing up), such as anti-adrenergics and alpha blockers, because these drugs can lead to fainting and falls, a common cause of hip fractures. Older adults should also avoid combination medications that contain alpha blockers, such as Labetalol. ACE inhibitors and angiotensin receptor blockers may also be appropriate in the elderly because of the high incidence of diabetes in this group.

- **People with heart disease.** People with stable angina and hypertension often benefit from beta blockers. The JNC recommends beta blockers for those who have had heart attacks because these medications reduce the risk of subsequent attacks. ACE inhibitors may also be prescribed after a heart attack.

- **People with congestive heart failure.** Because ACE inhibitors help prevent the progression of heart failure, the JNC recommends these drugs—either alone or in combination with a diuretic and/or an ARB—for people who have congestive heart failure and high blood pressure. Beta blockers may also be helpful.

- **People with left ventricular hypertrophy.** The JNC 7 found that all antihypertensive drugs except direct-acting vasodilators (Apresoline and Loniten) reduce left ventricle wall thickness. ACE inhibitors, however, are generally considered to be the most effective. Weight loss and salt restriction are also effective strategies for patients with this condition.

- **People with kidney disease.** People with kidney disease or diabetes respond favorably to ACE inhibitors and ARBs because these drugs can slow the rate of disease progression. But ACE inhibitors can promote a dangerous buildup of potassium, especially when taken with nonsteroidal anti-inflammatory drugs (NSAIDs) such as aspirin, ibuprofen, and many prescription painkillers. Consequently, potassium levels and kidney function tests must be closely monitored.

Over-the-Counter Medication

Always check with your doctor before taking over-the-counter drugs if you have hypertension. Many drugs, including some over-the-counter preparations, can elevate blood pressure. Hypertension may be a side effect of nasal decongestants, anabolic steroids, or MAO inhibitors (a class of antidepressants), as well as NSAIDs and COX-2 inhibitors, two popular classes of pain relievers. In addition, NSAIDs and COX-2 inhibitors can cause kidney dysfunction, especially in people at high risk for these problems, including people with hypertension.

The decongestants found in most over-the-counter cold, flu, and allergy medicines and many weight-loss supplements can elevate blood pressure and interfere with medications used to treat hypertension. The U.S. Food and Drug Administration banned one of the most common of these decongestants, phenyl-propanolamine, because it was linked to an increased risk of stroke, especially in women. Fortunately, some cold, cough, and flu remedies are specially formulated for people with high blood pressure. However, it's always a good idea to talk to your doctor and pharmacist before taking any over-the-counter medications.

Shortly after birth control pills came on the market in the 1960s, researchers discovered they raised blood pressure, sometimes to dangerously high levels. As a result, they were found to increase a woman's risk of stroke, particularly if she smoked.

However, these early oral contraceptives contained considerably higher doses of estrogen and progesterone than current formulations do. Today, it's much less common for oral contraceptives to cause hypertension, and when it does occur, it's usually among women who smoke, are obese, or are over thirty-five. In these cases, blood pressure usually returns to normal after the woman stops taking the pill.

Next Steps

We've covered all of the major tools available for preventing or controlling hypertension: stress management, diet, exercise, and—when necessary—medication. But we're not quite finished yet. We mentioned earlier that a tool is only as useful as your ability and willingness to use it. You might be a little overwhelmed, put off, or even intimidated about fitting any or all of these tools into your life, especially those that will be new to you. It can be a challenge to break old habits and begin new ones, even when you know that your health and well-being depend on it. The next chapter will help you find a way to incorporate these tools into your life.

CHAPTER 7

Bringing It All Together

Changing high-risk behaviors is often essential to well-being. Throughout this book, we have suggested a number of strategies that can help you lower your blood pressure. This chapter will help you take what you've learned and go that crucial extra step toward creating lasting change.

Understanding the Mechanics of Personal Change

Let's acknowledge something right off the bat: change doesn't come easily. Changes in lifestyle are often easy to initiate but notoriously difficult to sustain. People often embrace change with much enthusiasm, without truly understanding the long-term commitment and effort required. Changing behaviors is a complex process. Often, remaining stuck in a rut wins out as the lesser of two evils when compared to the prospect of breaking away from the familiar.

Research indicates that in order for change to be successful, it requires three steps:

1. Gathering information
2. Contemplating change and making a plan to implement it
3. Taking action on your plan and staying on track

In some cases and for some people, not all stages are necessary to create lasting change, but for most people, they are. Usually there is considerable overlap between one or more of these stages. Let's take a closer look at each stage so that we can better understand the important role they play in your personal change program.

Gathering Information

Like an attorney building a case, collecting factual information may be a logical first step for you. It might be a simple matter of learning your family history or your risk factors or something more complex, such as researching health publications or talking to your health care provider. While there are a few reputable sources of health information on the Internet, you should treat online information as a springboard for conversations with your health care provider rather than accept it as medical advice.

Gather the information necessary. Let's say that you're a smoker. You may, for example, find that your paternal grandfather was a smoker and that he also had hypertension. You can add to your knowledge base the fact that within hours of stopping smoking, your heart rate and blood pressure decrease; within a year of quitting, your heart disease risk is cut in half (within two to three years, your risk is equal to that of a nonsmoker).

Contemplating Change and Making a Plan to Implement It

Armed with your newfound facts, it should be relatively easy to build a well-reasoned case for change. You may want to start by making a list of all the reasons you want to change (the "pros"). Include all of the things that are likely to occur if you don't change. Next make a list of the reasons you don't want to change (the "cons"). What are some difficulties you might encounter along the way? Remember, we need to tip the scales in your favor. We need to make it more uncomfortable to continue on your current course than to create the change you need.

Before you take action on your decision to change, it's essential that you create a plan for doing so. Use imagery to see yourself with your healthier behaviors and notice how you feel. Your plan will serve as your road map to reaching your goal. Imagine trying to drive to a location you've never been to before, armed with only your best intentions. There is, of course, the odd chance that you'll make it to your destination, but why make it hard on yourself? Just as a map allows you to fulfill your intention to arrive at a new place, your plan for change empowers you with the steps and goals you'll need along the way.

The first step in creating your plan is to determine what's going to work for you and what's not. That means personalizing the plan to your specific likes and dislikes, schedule, current level of health and ability, budget, and any other factors that are important to you.

Inch by inch, everything's a cinch! Your next step in creating your plan is to set long- and short-term goals. Having only one vague goal can be overwhelming and counterproductive. Breaking your long-term goal into positive, measurable, and realistic short-term goals is especially important. For example, let's say your long-term goal is to lose five pounds in ten weeks. Broken down, that's an average of one-half pound per week. But maybe checking in every week feels a bit obsessive to you. Besides, you're likely to lose more weight some weeks than others. So let's say you'll check in with yourself every two weeks, a total of five times. Short-term goals not only keep you motivated to reach your ultimate destination, but they are also your best bet for picking up early warning signs that the approach you've chosen isn't working as well as it could. It happens. All the dedication in the world won't do much good if you're dealing with a faulty plan, just as a full tank of gas won't get you to Florida if you have a New England road map. If your plan for change involves multiple long-term goals (such as quitting smoking, exercising, and cutting back on salt), make sure to avoid trying for too much too soon.

Finally, you'll need to set a date to begin. In most cases, there's no time like the present. That little voice inside that says, "I'll start my diet tomorrow" or "I'll begin exercising next week when things quiet down a bit" is just the sort of defeating self-talk you must overcome in order to reach your goals. On the other hand, there are certain times in which it's wise to delay putting your plan into action. You may find yourself with an unusually heavy workload, in which case taking on any additional challenge would likely increase stress and lead to burnout. You may find yourself recovering from an illness or injury. The important thing is to recognize when you're only making excuses for yourself and when the need to forestall is legitimate.

Taking Action on Your Plan and Staying on Track

You've gotten all the facts; you've weighed the pros and cons; you've made a decision and a plan. Now it's time to get to it—no ifs, ands, or buts.

You may have heard it said that the journey of a thousand miles begins with one step. But how difficult that first step can be. That's because, as your eighth-grade science teacher told you, bodies at rest stay at rest until acted upon. In other words, you're fighting inertia when making that critical first step. But the good news is that bodies in motion tend to stay in motion, meaning that once you've begun, it becomes easier to continue, until it finally becomes a habit. Success begets success.

Getting on Track

Once you've begun working toward your goals, you can start to measure your performance. Keeping a journal or diary is a very powerful tool for helping you stay motivated and chart your progress. You may be as detailed as you like, even mentioning other things that are going on in your life so that you can see how factors such as stress or sleep levels may be affecting your progress. You may also like to include how you're feeling physically and emotionally with each entry. Include information on the relaxation response, exercise, and your home blood pressure readings.

Sample Plan to Quit Smoking

What I Know

1. Smoking can lead to hypertension, certain cancers, emphysema, and other serious health problems.
2. My mother, maternal grandfather, and brother suffered complications due to smoking.
3. I have smoked a pack and a half every day for the past fifteen years.
4. If I quit now, my risk of heart disease will be cut in half within a year.

Why I'm Going to Quit

1. I want to be around to see my kids get married.
2. I want to enjoy a better quality of life.
3. I'm tired of waking up in the middle of the night coughing.
4. I'm tired of smelling like smoke.
5. With all the money I've spent on smoking, I could have sent my kids to college.
6. I don't want to end up like my mother or grandfather.

How I'll Quit

1. Every time I get a craving, I'll consciously turn my thoughts to the negative consequences of smoking.
2. I'll avoid smoky bars and restaurants, where the smell might tempt me.
3. I'll join the smoking cessation group that's offered through my doctor's office.
4. I'll join that online support group I saw on the Internet.
5. I'll ask all my friends, family, and colleagues to support me.
6. I'll keep a quitting diary, where I record when cravings strike and how I handled them.
7. I'll reward each week of nonsmoking by having a nice dinner at my favorite restaurant or going to a movie.

Staying on Track

There will be times when the thrill of the chase toward your goal has faded, and your new maintenance phase wears thin. Even if you've successfully made your lifestyle changes into habits, you may find yourself tempted to "cheat" from time to time. You may even find yourself rationalizing, "I've lost ten pounds; I deserve to cheat on my diet." The key to successful behavior change is moderation, not deprivation. But ask yourself—and be honest, of course—if this isn't the same kind of thinking that brought you those ten extra pounds in the first place. (And it should go without saying that "cheating" is simply not an option for someone who has broken an addiction to alcohol, nicotine, or other drugs.)

On the other hand, let's face it, life happens. You're only human. You had a really bad day at work and when you get home, you decide to eat a big bowl of ice cream instead of taking a walk. Like we said, the first reaction to change tends to be resistance. It can take a couple of attempts to get on track and stay there for good, and occasional lapses in behavior are normal; they might even be good opportunities for learning and growth, if you handle them the right way.

So when you see yourself slipping, take some time to review the situation. Let go of negative feelings and judgments. Practicing mindfulness can help you recognize lapses more easily. The important thing is not to beat yourself up—after all, it's better to experience a setback when trying to do something positive than to be perfectly successful at maintaining your bad habits.

Some degree of setback or even frustration with the challenges of creating change is almost inevitable. One thing you might try to do is to plan to take on new changes gradually. You'll also want to avoid being unnecessarily rigid with your plan. Things may pop up every now and then that will get in the way of your goal. It's important to have a "plan B" and to be flexible about revising your plan as necessary.

There's often a tendency to peg yourself as a saint or a sinner when it comes to attempts at change. That is, positive feelings about your progress toward change come only when you are in

100 percent compliance with the standards you've set for yourself, and the slightest slip is enough to make you label yourself a failure. By now you should be able to recognize that kind of thinking for what it is—the "all-or-nothing" thinking we discussed in Chapter 3.

As you'll remember, cognitive distortions are negative thinking patterns that have a particular knack for snowballing, consuming your thoughts, and negatively affecting mood and emotion. You'll also remember that deflating a cognitive distortion is often a matter of taking four simple steps: stop, breathe, reflect, and choose. (For a more detailed explanation, refer to Chapter 3.)

Wrapping Up

There's an old story about a man who was celebrating his hundredth birthday. He had become something of a celebrity in his small town, so on the day he officially became a centenarian, a reporter from the local newspaper visited him at home to discover the key to his impressive longevity. When asked what his secret was, the old man took a moment to ponder and then said, "Well, I never smoked, and I never drank. I watched what I ate, and I got plenty of exercise."

The young reporter scribbled the man's words down on his notepad, then replied, "Interesting. But my grandfather did all of those things, and he lived to be only seventy-five. How do you explain that?" Without missing a beat, the old man said, "That's easy. He didn't keep it up long enough!"

It's a lighthearted story, but the message is simple: keep it up. Keep it up because you know that it's good for your health. Keep it up because you want to live life to the fullest. Keep it up because you know that you can. Throughout this book, our solitary goal has been to teach you to change your health and well-being for the better. But as Galileo said, one cannot teach people anything; you can only help them find it inside themselves. The real change is yours to make. The real tools are not found in the pages of this book; they are—as they always have been—inside you, waiting to be tapped.

Congratulate yourself for making it this far. Refer to this book anytime you need a refresher or a "tune-up." Remember, the path to success is rarely a straight line. Accept the inevitable ups and downs as a necessary part of the process.

Your journey toward better health is just beginning, and we'd like to thank you for letting us be a part of it.

Appendix A

Additional Relaxation Response Exercises

Here are some scripts that we use in our clinic that can be used in addition to the relaxation response exercises in Chapter 3. You can either practice these scripts on your own or consider purchasing a tape or CD from the M/BMI website (mbmi.org).

For each exercise, choose a quiet spot where you will not be disturbed. Sit or lie down in a comfortable position. Take a few deep breaths, settling comfortably into the chair or on the floor. Assume a passive attitude. Don't worry about how well you are performing the exercise.

Safe Place

Assume a comfortable position either lying down or sitting in a chair. Take a few slow, deep breaths. When you feel quiet, continue as follows:

Imagine a beautiful light centered over your heart. As you look into the light, you notice a scene developing that you recognize as a place of special meaning to you. It is a safe place, a place where you feel comfortable, relaxed, and at peace. It could be a place you remember from childhood, a place you know as an adult, or an imaginary place that you know would provide you with security and comfort. Allow yourself to settle into this safe place. Find a comfortable position and let your body relax; let your senses take in the surroundings. What do you see, smell, hear, feel? Focus your awareness on the moment, on being with yourself, feeling peaceful. If you notice your mind drifting toward thoughts or concerns of the past or future, watch these thoughts without judgment, then gently let them go and bring your awareness back to the essence of your safe place. Use your breath or a repetitive word or phrase to anchor your awareness in the moment as you simply settle into the comfort and peacefulness of this special place.

Now it's time to begin to shift your awareness from your safe place to the environment around you. But before you leave your special place, pay attention to how it felt to feel safe and secure, free of stress and conflict, so that when you recognize increasing stress in your everyday life, you will have the memory of feeling peaceful and quiet and can shift your thoughts to a safe focus in the present moment. Begin to pay attention to the sensations around you. Open your eyes, stretch, and begin to move in a slow, gentle manner, paying attention to how it feels to move. Watch your thoughts as you transition back to your surroundings.

Special Place

Before beginning this relaxation, think of a place where you feel comfortable, relaxed, and at ease. It can be inside or outdoors, maybe a room in your home or on a beach. This can be a place you have visited or seen a picture of, or it can be a place you create right now.

Now that you have a relaxing place in mind, settle in and spend the next few minutes allowing all of your senses to be fully present. If other noises interfere, you can notice them, then let them go and return your thoughts to relaxed concentration.

Count from ten back to one slowly, becoming aware of your breath. Breathe in awareness and breathe out tension. Feel how your breath moves down to your belly. Breathe in a feeling of quiet and calm. Let your exhalation release any tension or stress. Settle into a comfortale position.

Now think of a relaxing, warm light, such as the sun, passing over you. It goes down from the top of your head, warming and relaxing your eyes and your cheeks, down to your jaw. The light moves down your neck, warming and releasing any tension there, next warming your shoulders and releasing tension as you continue to breathe in feelings of calmness and peacefulness and breathe out tension.

The warmth relaxes down your shoulders, moving down your fingers, allowing tension to release from your fingertips. The light then moves down your upper back to your lower back, down to your legs and your toes, where tension is released and washed away through the floor, leaving you relaxed and calm.

As you continue to breathe gently and calmly in easy, comfortable breaths, become aware again of entering and being in your special place. Notice what you see around you, if there are any sounds or any familiar smells. If you're indoors, you might notice details about the space you're in, such as the way light falls. If you're outdoors, you might notice if there's a breeze or the temperature of the air around you.

Whatever you need is here, because you've created this space. If you want to sit down and rest, there might be a soft chair if you're inside or a hammock if you're outdoors.

Appreciate the comfort here, how safe it is, breathing in a sense of calm and relaxation, breathing out tension. You can return to this place whenever you need to relax.

To end this guided relaxation count from ten to one. At ten, gently become aware of your breath; at nine, notice how rested your body feels. At seven and eight, begin to slowly stretch and transition back to the present. At six, think of the room you are sitting in. At five and four, notice any sounds in the room. At three, begin stretching. At two, slowly open your eyes, and at one, return to the room you're in, feeling relaxed, contented, and with a sense of accomplishment in what you have just experienced.

Beach

Imagine yourself standing on a staircase ten steps above a beautiful beach. Go down a few steps, becoming aware of a few bits of sand under your feet. Slowly take a few more steps, becoming aware of a breeze against your skin. Walk down to the fifth step, where you feel the sun against your back; a few more steps and you hear the ocean. When you get to the bottom, step onto the sand and begin to walk slowly toward the water, being aware of all your senses—smell, sound, touch. Walk to the water and look over it, noting the color, the sound of waves, the feel of sand under your feet, the feel of the sun against your skin and the breeze against your face. Immerse all of your senses in this experience. Walk slowly up and down the beach, noting all the sensations.

After five to ten minutes, take a last slow look at the water, then walk back toward the steps. Climb the steps slowly, one at a time, noting the sensations from the beach getting dimmer. At the top of the stairs, refocus slowly to the sounds around you.

Garden

In your mind's eye, begin to see yourself in a special garden, one that you know well, one that you remember, or one that you create in your mind. Become aware of the flowers—their shape and colors. Notice the trees and the sunlight as it comes down through the branches. What are the smells and aromas in your garden? Feel the fresh air against your cheeks. As you walk through this garden, notice the ground beneath your feet—is it grass or dirt or cobblestone? Notice how good you feel in this place.

As you walk along your path, you come to a patch of earth that is waiting to be planted. Near this spot is a small shovel and a bag of seeds. With your hands on the shovel, you begin to dig a hole; notice the texture of the soil, its color, its smell. When you're ready, pick up a handful of seeds and notice how these seeds feel in your hand. The seeds are new goals, affirmations, or something you want for yourself. From a space of open acceptance, allow that goal or wish to come into your mind without any critical judgment or editing. Allow images to surface. Take your time to explore the choices. Now plant the seeds that represent these goals and wishes. Gradually cover them with soil, patting them very carefully. On your right is a watering can. Use it to give the seeds some water. Take time to relax in the garden. Perhaps there is a bench nearby, or you can lie down on the grass.

Now you can let your seeds take root, knowing that they have everything they need to grow, safe in the garden of your mind.

When you are ready, slowly walk out of your imaginary garden, experiencing the colors, the sunlight, and the smells and realizing how good you feel there.

Autogenic Training

Autogenic training focuses on your body and on feeling the parts of your body as warm and heavy. If necessary, you may record this script. Assume a comfortable position. Begin by taking a few slow, deep breaths to relax you. Slowly say to yourself, "I am beginning to feel very quiet. . . . I am beginning to feel relaxed. . . . My feet, knees, and hips feel heavy. . . . Heaviness and warmth are flowing through my feet and legs. . . . My hands, arms, and shoulders feel heavy. . . . Warmth and heaviness are flowing through my hands and arms. . . . My neck, jaw, tongue, and forehead feel relaxed and smooth. . . . My whole body feels quiet, heavy, and comfortable. . . . I am comfortably relaxed. . . . Warmth and heaviness flow into my arms, hands, and fingertips. . . . My breathing is slow and regular. . . . I am aware of my calm, regular heartbeat. . . . My mind is becoming quieter as I focus inward. . . . I feel still. . . . Deep in my mind I experience myself as relaxed, comfortable, and still. I am alert in a quiet, inward way."

As you finish your relaxation, take in several deep, reenergizing breaths, bringing light and energy into every cell of your body. Go about your day feeling energized and refreshed.

Appendix B

Heart-Healthy Recipes

The following collection of recipes is intended to be easy and user-friendly. The recipes are generally low in saturated fats, trans fats, cholesterol, and sodium, as well as low-fat. They are high in nutrients, vitamins, and minerals such as potassium, calcium, and fiber. Recipes are included for breakfasts; appetizers and snacks; salads; marinades, sauces, and dressings; entrees; and desserts.

Breakfast Recipes

You've probably heard that breakfast is the most important meal of the day, which makes it curious to think that so many people choose sugary cereal, fatty bacon or sausage, or even a donut or Danish to start the morning off. Breakfast should be healthy and satisfying—and it can be. The following recipes are simple and delicious, and some can even be made ahead of time for quick and easy morning preparation.

Scrambled Tofu

Makes 4 1-cup servings

Olive oil
½ cup diced onion
1 teaspoon turmeric
1 pound extra-firm tofu, drained and crumbled
6 tomatoes, chopped
½ cup diced zucchini
½ cup diced mushrooms
½ cup diced red bell pepper
3 tablespoons Mrs. Dash 10-Minute Marinade, southwestern
    chipotle flavor
Dash of Tabasco sauce

Heat about 1 tablespoon olive oil in large skillet. Sauté onion and turmeric until translucent. Add in tofu and other vegetables. Continue to sauté until tofu is slightly brown and vegetables are cooked. Mix well with Mrs. Dash marinade and Tabasco sauce.

Nutrition information per serving: calories: 150, fat: 8 g, saturated fat: 1 g, total carbs: 20 g, fiber: 4 g, sodium: 20 mg, protein: 8 g

Pepper Chicken Frittata

Makes 2 6- to 8-ounce servings

1 cup chopped green peppers
½ cup chopped cooked chicken
¼ cup finely chopped tomato
½ medium onion, chopped fine
½ teaspoon dried Italian seasoning
⅛ teaspoon salt
1 cup egg substitute

Preheat broiler. Spray a medium skillet with an ovenproof handle with nonstick cooking spray; heat over medium heat. Add peppers, chicken, tomato, onion, Italian seasoning, and salt; cook 3 minutes, or until pepper is crisp-tender, stirring occasionally. Add egg substitute. Reduce heat to low; cover. Cook 9 minutes, or until bottom of frittata is set but top is still slightly moist. Remove lid from skillet. Place skillet under broiler. Broil 2 minutes, or until top is set but not brown. Cut frittata in half to serve.

Nutrition information per serving: calories: 130, fat: 1.5 g, saturated fat: 1 g, cholesterol: 45 mg, total carbs: 3 g, fiber: 1 g, sodium: 275 mg, protein: 25 g

Summer Vegetable Strata

Makes 4 6- to 8-ounce servings

> 1 medium onion, chopped
> 1 small zucchini, sliced
> 1 small red or green bell pepper, chopped fine
> 2 cups whole-wheat (1-inch) bread cubes
> ⅓ cup shredded low-fat mozzarella cheese
> Dash Tabasco sauce
> 1 cup egg substitute
> ¾ cup skim milk
> ¼ teaspoon ground black pepper

Spray an 8-inch square baking dish with cooking spray; set aside. Spray a large skillet with cooking spray; heat over medium-high heat. Cook onion, zucchini, and bell peppers 6 minutes, or until vegetables are crisp-tender, stirring occasionally. Add bread cubes; mix lightly. Spoon into prepared baking dish. Sprinkle with cheese and Tabasco sauce. Beat egg substitute, milk, and black pepper in a medium bowl with a wire whisk until well blended; pour over bread mixture. Cover. Refrigerate at least 30 minutes or overnight.

Preheat oven to 375°F. Uncover strata and bake 50 minutes, or until top is golden brown and a knife inserted in the center comes out clean. Let stand 10 minutes before cutting into four squares to serve.

Nutrition information per serving: calories: 155, fat: 5 g, saturated fat: 2 g, total carbs: 16 g, fiber: 4 g, sodium: 295 mg, protein: 12 g

Oat and Molasses Banana Bread

Makes 14 slices

1 cup all-purpose flour
½ cup whole-wheat flour
⅔ cup old-fashioned oats
1 teaspoon baking soda
1 teaspoon ground cinnamon
¼ teaspoon salt
⅔ cup sugar
⅛ cup butter, softened
⅛ cup canola oil
⅓ cup dark molasses
1 cup egg substitute
⅓ cup plain nonfat yogurt
2 ripe bananas, mashed
1 teaspoon vanilla extract

Preheat oven to 350°F. Combine flours with oats, baking soda, cinnamon, and salt, stirring with a whisk. Beat sugar, butter, oil, and molasses in a large bowl at medium speed for 1 minute. Add egg substitute little by little, while continuing to beat. Add yogurt, bananas, and vanilla; beat until blended. Add flour mixture, and beat until just moist. Spoon batter into an 8½″ × 4½″ loaf pan coated with cooking spray. Bake for an hour, or until a toothpick inserted in the center comes out clean. Cool on a wire rack.

Nutrition information per serving (1 slice): calories: 175, fat: 4 g, saturated fat: 1 g, total carbs: 32 g, fiber: 2 g, sodium: 200 mg, protein: 3 g

Whole-Wheat Apple Muffins ✓

Makes 12 muffins

1 cup white pastry flour
½ cup whole-wheat flour
2 teaspoons baking powder
¾ teaspoon baking soda
½ cup egg substitute
⅓ cup sugar
⅓ cup canola oil
¾ cup fat-free buttermilk
½ teaspoon vanilla
1½ cups peeled, cored, and finely chopped apples

Preheat oven to 400°F. Insert paper liners in miniature muffin tins, or spray with nonstick cooking spray, and set aside. In a large bowl, combine pastry flour, whole-wheat flour, baking powder, and baking soda. Stir in the egg substitute, sugar, oil, buttermilk, vanilla, and apples just until combined; do not overmix. Spoon mixture into prepared muffin tins, filling about ¾ full. Bake in center of oven for 15 minutes, or until muffins are firm and a toothpick inserted in the center of a muffin comes out clean. Remove muffins from pan and cool on a wire rack. Serve warm or cool.

Nutrition information per serving (1 muffin): calories: 167, fat: 6 g, saturated fat: 0 g, total carbs: 25 g, fiber: 1.25 g, sodium: 175 mg, protein: 4 g

Whole-Grain Pancakes

Makes 14 pancakes

¾ cup all-purpose flour

¾ cup whole-wheat flour

3 tablespoons turbinado sugar or brown sugar

½ teaspoon salt

2 teaspoons baking powder

¼ teaspoon ground nutmeg

1 cup egg substitute

3 tablespoons canola oil

1½ cups skim milk (or soy milk or rice milk)

1 teaspoon vanilla

Mix dry ingredients in a medium bowl. In a second bowl, combine egg substitute, oil, milk, and vanilla, beating well. Pour mixture over dry ingredients and stir just enough to combine. For each pancake, pour ¼ cup batter onto a nonstick griddle or skillet set over medium-high heat. Cook a few minutes, without disturbing, until fine bubbles appear over the surface. Flip the pancakes over and cook until browned on the second side, about 1 minute. When done, remove to a platter and serve right away, or keep warm in a 200°F oven until all pancakes are finished.

For **buttermilk pancakes**, use 1½ cups buttermilk in place of skim milk and add 1 teaspoon baking soda. If you don't have buttermilk, add 1 tablespoon vinegar to 1 cup milk and let stand for 10 minutes. It will curdle slightly.

For **flaxseed pancakes**, add ¼ cup flaxseed meal (ground flaxseed) to recipe. If batter is too thick, thin with extra milk. (Flaxseed meal is a good source of heart-healthy omega-3 fats and soluble fiber, which may lower LDL levels.)

Nutrition information per serving (1 medium pancake): calories: 105, fat: 3 g, saturated fat: 0 g, total carbs: 14 g, fiber: 1 g, sodium: 130 mg, protein: 4 g

Appetizers and Snacks

These recipes make great appetizers but are also simple and portable enough to use as quick snacks at home or work.

Yogurt "Cheese" ✓

Makes approximately 1½ to 2 cups

1 32-ounce container plain nonfat yogurt

Line a colander or strainer with cheesecloth or two to three layers of paper coffee filters. Place colander in a bowl. Spoon yogurt into center of colander. Cover with plastic wrap and let sit overnight in the refrigerator (the longer it sits, the firmer the "cheese" will be). Store in an airtight container in the refrigerator.

Yogurt cheese keeps well in the refrigerator for up to 1 week. It can be served as a dip or spread with crackers and veggies or be used in recipes in place of cream cheese.

Nutrition information per serving (2 tablespoons): calories: 50, fat: 0 g, saturated fat: 0 g, fiber: 0 g, sodium: 30 mg, protein: 10 g

Herbed Yogurt "Cheese"

Makes approximately 1½ to 2 cups

- 1 32-ounce container plain nonfat yogurt
- 1 tablespoon olive oil
- 3 garlic cloves, minced
- 3 tablespoons minced fresh parsley
- 1 tablespoon minced fresh dill
- ½ teaspoon dried rosemary
- ½ teaspoon dried basil
- ½ teaspoon dried thyme

Line a colander or strainer with cheesecloth or two to three layers of paper coffee filters. Place colander in a bowl. Spoon yogurt into center of colander. Cover with plastic wrap and let sit overnight in the refrigerator (the longer it sits, the firmer the "cheese" will become, to the consistency of soft cream cheese). Mix in remaining ingredients. Stir well. Store in an airtight container in the refrigerator.

Nutrition information per serving (2 tablespoons): calories: 70, fat: 2 g, saturated fat: 0 g, total carbs: 5–10 g, fiber: 0 g, sodium: 30 mg, protein: 10 g

Crispy Garlic Tofu Bites

Makes 4 servings

4 teaspoons tamari

6 cloves garlic, minced

2½ tablespoons lemon juice

½ cup orange juice concentrate

½ cup tamarind paste or tomato paste

½ cup salt-free ketchup

1 tablespoon minced fresh ginger (use a 1-inch piece)

½ teaspoon curry powder

½ teaspoon garam masala or allspice

1½ tablespoons molasses

4 teaspoons cornstarch

1 tablespoon cold water

1 pound extra-firm tofu, with water squeezed out

4 teaspoons canola oil

1 cup sunflower seeds, toasted

Combine tamari, garlic, lemon juice, orange juice, tamarind paste, ketchup, ginger, curry powder, garam masala, and molasses in a small saucepan. Bring to a rolling simmer. Combine cornstarch and cold water. While sauce simmers slowly, whisk in diluted cornstarch. Simmer sauce for 1 minute; remove pan from heat. When tofu is ready, cut into 1-inch squares, coat in marinade mixed with canola oil, and marinate for 2 hours in the refrigerator.

Preheat oven to 400°F. Roll tofu in sunflower seeds until well coated. Place on a lightly oiled baking pan. Bake for about 25 minutes, or until deep golden brown, turning the pan once during cooking.

Nutrition information per serving: calories: 110, fat: 6 g, saturated fat: 0 g, total carbs: 5 g, fiber: 0 g, sodium: 250 mg, protein: 10 g

Healthy Trail Mix

Makes 20–25 ½-cup servings

- 1 box of any whole-grain cereal
- ½ cup walnuts or almonds
- 1 cup unsalted soy nuts
- 2 cups mixed dried fruit (raisins, cranberries, and so on)

Mix all ingredients and store in an airtight jar. (You can also add flaxseed meal to this trail mix for its heart-healthy omega-3 and fiber benefits.)

Nutrition information per serving: calories: 150, fat: 5 g, saturated fat: 1 g, total carbs: 20 g, fiber: 5 g, sodium: 23 mg, protein: 6 g

hickpea Spread/Dip

:ups

6-ounce can chickpeas, drained and rinsed
2 tablespoons light mayonnaise
1 small tomato, diced
1 clove garlic, crushed
2 teaspoons lemon juice
⅛ to ½ teaspoon cayenne pepper
¼ to 1 teaspoon ground cumin
⅛ to ¼ teaspoon turmeric
2 teaspoons chopped fresh parsley
4 whole-wheat pita pockets, toasted and cut in half if desired

Placed rinsed chickpeas in a bowl, and mash to a pulp with a fork. (A food processor also works well.) Add remaining ingredients except pita, and mix to form a thick and creamy spread. Serve on whole-wheat pita pockets. Add sliced tomato, cucumber, or onion if desired.

Nutrition information per serving (½ cup without pita pocket):
calories: 330, fat: 5 g, saturated fat: 0 g, total carbs: 63 g, fiber: 8 g, sodium: 200 mg, protein: 8 g

Salads

If the word *salad* conjures up images of wilted iceberg lettuce with a dab of tasteless dressing, then you're in for a surprise. These salads are low in calories and are good sources of fiber and protein.

Tofu Egg Salad

Makes 4–6 ½-cup servings

- 1 16-ounce package extra-firm tofu
- 1 tablespoon prepared mustard
- 1 tablespoon honey
- 2 tablespoons soy mayonnaise or low-fat mayonnaise
- 1 tablespoon white vinegar
- ½ teaspoon turmeric
- 1 teaspoon onion powder
- 1 teaspoon celery seed
- ½ teaspoon ground black pepper
- ¼ cup minced celery
- ¼ cup minced green pepper

Drain tofu and crumble. Combine mustard, honey, mayonnaise, vinegar, turmeric, onion powder, celery seed, pepper, minced celery, and minced green pepper. Mix well. Pour over crumbled tofu and toss well. Serve chilled.

Nutrition information per serving: calories: 90, fat: 4 g, saturated fat: 0.5 g, total carbs: 7 g, fiber: 2 g, sodium: 65 mg, protein: 7 g

Black Bean and Couscous Salad ✓

Makes 4 1- to 1½-cup servings

1 cup whole-wheat couscous

2 cups boiling water

1½ cups frozen yellow corn

2 cups cooked black beans (if using canned beans, drain and
　　rinse)

1 small onion, chopped

2 scallions, sliced

16 cherry tomatoes, halved

4 garlic cloves, minced

½ habanero pepper, minced

¼ cup chopped fresh cilantro leaves

1 teaspoon ground cumin

2 tablespoons Mrs. Dash Southwestern Chipotle Sauce

Put couscous in a large bowl and add boiling water. Cover. When water has been absorbed (about 20 minutes), add frozen corn and mix. (The heat from the couscous will thaw the corn.) Add remaining ingredients and mix well.

Nutrition information per serving: calories: 275, fat: 1 g, saturated fat: 0 g, total carbs: 62 g, fiber: 12 g, sodium: 200 mg, protein: 13 g

Edamame Salad with Herbs

Makes 4 1-cup servings

1 16-ounce bag organic shelled edamame
4 large garlic cloves, chopped
1 tablespoon olive oil
1 cup plain nonfat yogurt
¼ cup chopped fresh flat-leaf parsley
2 tablespoons finely diced red bell pepper
1 tablespoon thinly sliced fresh basil
2 teaspoon balsamic vinegar
Bibb or Boston lettuce leaves for serving

Boil edamame in salted water to cover until tender, about 5 minutes. Drain. Mix with remaining ingredients. Serve salad on lettuce leaves.

Nutrition information per serving: calories: 210, fat: 11 g, saturated fat: 1 g, total carbs: 14 g, fiber: 5 g, sodium: 60 mg, protein: 14 g

Strawberry-Spinach Salad

Makes 4 1-cup servings

4 cups spinach leaves
2 cups halved strawberries
2 tablespoons sugar
2 tablespoons balsamic vinegar
¼ teaspoon ground black pepper

Wash spinach leaves under cool running water; pat dry, remove stems, and tear into bite-size pieces. Place torn spinach in a large bowl; cover and chill. Combine strawberries, sugar, and vinegar in a small bowl; toss gently. Cover and chill at least 2 hours, stirring occasionally. Add strawberry mixture and pepper to torn spinach; toss well. Serve immediately.

Nutrition information per serving: calories: 50, fat: 0.3 g, saturated fat: 0 g, total carbs: 12 g, fiber: 4 g, sodium: 15 mg, protein: 1 g

Summer Salad with Flaxseed Vinaigrette

Makes 4 1- to 1½-cup servings

2 tablespoons flaxseed oil

¼ cup balsamic vinegar

3 tablespoons chopped fresh basil leaves

2 teaspoons organic Dijon mustard

1 clove garlic, chopped

¼ teaspoon salt

⅛ teaspoon ground black pepper

2 cups baby spinach

3 cups arugula

1 pint cherry tomatoes

½ cup slivered red onion

1 avocado, cut into ½-inch cubes

In a small jar, combine flaxseed oil, vinegar, basil, mustard, garlic, salt, and pepper. Cover and shake until well combined. In a large salad bowl, combine spinach, arugula, tomatoes, red onion, avocado, and dressing. Toss to combine.

Nutrition information per serving: calories: 150, fat: 10 g, saturated fat: 2.5 g, total carbs: 12 g, fiber: 4 g, sodium: 240 mg, protein: 3g

Low-Sodium Marinades, Sauces, and Dressings

It's quick and easy to make your own fresh dressings and marinades, which are tastier and healthier than most bottled varieties. You can easily mix these up ahead of time and even double or triple the recipe portions. Store them in an airtight bottle or container for future use.

Mixed Herb Garlic

Makes 1 cup

6 cloves garlic, chopped
⅓ cup chopped fresh thyme
¼ cup chopped fresh rosemary
2 tablespoons chopped fresh basil
¼ cup lemon juice
¼ cup balsamic vinegar
½ cup olive oil
½ teaspoon ground black pepper

Ginger Peanut

Makes 1 cup

½ cup vegetable broth
½ cup creamy peanut butter
1 tablespoon tamari
1 teaspoon chopped fresh ginger
2 tablespoons rice wine vinegar
2 teaspoons honey
½ teaspoon cayenne pepper

Shallot Mustard

Makes 1 cup

¾ cup balsamic vinegar

½ cup olive oil

3 tablespoons prepared mustard

4 garlic cloves, chopped

½ teaspoon ground black pepper

1 teaspoon roasted ground cumin

2 teaspoons chopped shallots

Tex-Mex

Makes 1 cup

½ cup grapefruit juice

¼ cup lime juice

¼ cup honey

2 teaspoons ground cumin

3 garlic cloves, chopped

2 jalapeño peppers, seeded and chopped

¼ teaspoon Tabasco sauce

¼ cup chopped fresh cilantro

Entrees

Why bother with a frozen dinner or other prepackaged food when a heart-healthy entree is quick, simple, and inexpensive to make? These entrees also make great leftovers for lunches, and most of them keep well in the freezer.

Tofu Parmigiana

Makes 4 servings

½ cup bread crumbs

4 tablespoons Parmesan cheese, divided

2 teaspoons dried oregano, divided

Ground black pepper to taste

1 12-ounce package extra-firm tofu

2 tablespoons olive oil

1 12-ounce can no-added-salt tomato sauce

½ teaspoon dried basil

1 clove garlic, minced

½ cup shredded part-skim mozzarella cheese

Preheat oven to 400°F. In a small bowl, combine bread crumbs, 2 tablespoons Parmesan cheese, 1 teaspoon oregano, and black pepper. Slice tofu into ¼-inch-thick slices. One at a time, press tofu slices into crumb mixture, turning to coat all sides. Heat oil in a medium skillet over medium heat. Cook tofu slices until crisp on one side. Drizzle with a bit more olive oil, turn, and brown on the other side. Combine tomato sauce, basil, garlic, and remaining oregano. Place a thin layer of sauce in an 8-inch square baking pan. Arrange tofu slices in pan. Spoon remaining sauce over tofu. Top with shredded mozzarella and remaining Parmesan. Bake for 20 minutes.

Nutrition information per serving: calories: 212, fat: 15 g, saturated fat: 4 g, total carbs: 2 g, fiber: 0 g, sodium: 240 mg, protein: 17 g

BBQ Tempeh on Whole-Wheat Couscous

Makes 4 servings

1 pound tempeh, cut into 8 slices
1 cup Mrs. Dash Mesquite Grill Marinade
¼ teaspoon each salt, ground black pepper, and garlic power
2 tablespoons olive oil
1 cup uncooked whole-wheat couscous
¼ cup minced parsley

Preheat oven to 400°F. Coat tempeh completely with marinade, salt, pepper, garlic powder, and olive oil. Place in an 8-inch square baking dish. Bake for 30 minutes. Meanwhile, cook the couscous according to package directions. To serve, place ½ cup of cooked couscous on a plate, top with 2 slices of tempeh, and garnish with parsley.

Nutrition information per serving: calories: 300, fat: 9 g, saturated fat: 1 g, total carbs: 40 g, fiber: 3 g, sodium: 150 mg, protein: 12 g

Vegetarian Chili

Makes 6 1-cup servings

2 to 3 large zucchini or summer squash, chopped

2 medium onions, diced

3 tablespoons olive oil

2 sweet red peppers, cubed

2 large carrots, grated

4 garlic cloves, minced

1 28-ounce can low-sodium Italian tomatoes, cut up

1 can kidney beans, drained and rinsed

1 12-ounce package soy crumbles

1 6-ounce can no-added-salt tomato sauce or paste

1 teaspoon sugar

2 tablespoons chili powder

1 teaspoon cumin

1 teaspoon oregano

¼ teaspoon cayenne pepper

3 cups cooked brown rice

In large saucepan sauté zucchini and onion in olive oil until tender. Add red pepper, carrots, and garlic, and continue to sauté for 5 minutes. Add chopped tomatoes, kidney beans, soy crumbles, tomato sauce, sugar, and spices. Simmer until cooked thoroughly, about 20 to 30 minutes, stirring occasionally. Serve over brown rice.

Nutrition information per serving (without rice): calories: 200, fat: 10 g, saturated fat: 1 g, total carbs: 16 g, fiber: 18 g, sodium: 200 mg, protein: 10 g

Meatless Italian Pasta Sauce

Makes 6–8 ½-cup servings

4 tablespoons olive oil
1 medium onion, chopped
1½ heaping tablespoons chopped garlic
1 rounded tablespoon fennel seeds
1 12-ounce package soy crumbles
1 28-ounce can ground, peeled, no-added-salt Italian tomatoes
2 6-ounce cans no-added-salt tomato paste
2 cups water
¼ cup chopped parsley
7 to 10 shakes Tabasco sauce
Whole-wheat pasta to serve

Pour olive oil into a large saucepan. Add chopped onion. Add chopped garlic and fennel seeds. Sauté ingredients for about 5 to 6 minutes. Add soy crumbles and sauté for another 5 minutes. Add tomatoes. Mix in tomato paste and water, and stir. Add chopped parsley and Tabasco sauce. Let simmer for about 1 hour, stirring at intervals. Serve with ½ cup whole-wheat pasta.

Instead of the tomatoes and tomato paste, you can use 1 24- to 26-ounce jar of ready no-added-salt pasta sauce.

Nutrition information per serving (with pasta): calories: 350, fat: 13 g, saturated fat: 0 g, total carbs: 45 g, fiber: 5 g, sodium: 210 mg, protein: 12 g

Italian Meatballs (Veggie Balls) ✓

Makes approximately 10 meatballs

1 12-ounce package soy crumbles or ground turkey meat
2 tablespoons chopped garlic
1 small onion, diced fine
¼ cup chopped parsley
½ cup egg substitute
¼ cup Parmesan cheese or grated soy cheese
1 rounded tablespoon ground black pepper
¼ cup bread crumbs
Whole-wheat pasta to serve

Preheat oven to 375°F. In a small mixing bowl, combine crumbles, garlic, onion, parsley, egg substitute, cheese, pepper, and bread crumbs. Knead all ingredients together, mixing thoroughly. Roll into small to medium balls. Place on a cookie sheet that has been sprayed with olive oil to prevent sticking, making sure that balls don't touch each other. Bake for 40 minutes until firm and crusted. Serve on top of whole-wheat pasta covered with any pasta sauce.

Nutrition information per serving (2 meatballs, without pasta): calories: 280, fat: 5 g, saturated fat: 2 g, total carbs: 45 g, fiber: 5 g, sodium: 210 mg, protein: 12 g

Quinoa Pilaf

Makes 6–8 1-cup servings

½ cup diced carrot
½ cup diced green onion
¼ cup diced green pepper
¼ cup diced sweet red pepper
¼ cup diced celery
¼ cup olive oil
¼ teaspoon oregano
2 cloves garlic, crushed
6 cups quinoa, cooked per recipe on box
Salt to taste
1 cup almonds, sliced
Squeeze of lemon juice

Sauté chopped vegetables in olive oil until clear yet crisp. Stir in oregano and garlic. Add sautéed vegetables to cooked, hot quinoa, mixing well. Add salt to taste. Toast almonds in a heavy skillet until lightly golden. Add almonds and lemon juice to quinoa mixture, mixing well. Serve as a side dish with fish or chicken.

Vary the pilaf using your favorite vegetables, or by cooking the quinoa in chicken, fish, or vegetable stock instead of water. (This may slightly increase the sodium content of the dish.)

Nutrition information per serving: calories: 400, fat: 10 g, saturated fat: 1 g, total carbs: 65 g, fiber: 10 g, sodium: 12 mg (without added salt), protein: 15 g

Saag Chhole (Indian Spinach and Chickpea Curry)

Makes 6 ½-cup servings

2 tablespoons canola oil

1 teaspoon whole cumin seeds

2 onions, chopped

2 teaspoons fresh chopped ginger

1 tablespoon fresh chopped garlic

1 teaspoon cayenne pepper

2 teaspoons curry powder

1 teaspoon garam masala or allspice

4 plum tomatoes, chopped

1 large bunch fresh, or 1 pound frozen, spinach

1 16-ounce can chickpeas, drained and rinsed

Heat oil in a pan. Add cumin seeds and onion, and fry till light brown. Add ginger and garlic. After 1 minute, add cayenne, curry powder, garam masala, and chopped tomatoes. Cook for about 5 minutes. Add spinach; cook until it is completely soft and wilted and all the water has dried up. Add chickpeas and mix well; simmer for 5 minutes before serving. Serve as a filling for whole-wheat wraps.

You can also add 1 cup water and make a curry/gravy (don't let all the water dry up), and serve it over brown rice or whole-wheat couscous.

Nutrition information per serving: calories: 240, fat: 12 g, saturated fat: 0 g, total carbs: 25 g, fiber: 9 g, sodium: 150 mg, protein: 7 g

Tempting Tempeh Stir-Fry

Makes 5–6 1-cup servings

1 8-ounce package tempeh, sliced in ¼-inch strips
3 tablespoons low-sodium tamari sauce
4 garlic cloves, minced
2 teaspoons minced fresh ginger
1 bunch scallions, chopped
2 tablespoons canola oil
2 carrots, sliced
2 stalks celery, chopped
2 cups broccoli florets
1 green bell pepper, chopped
1 red bell pepper, chopped
3 cups cooked brown rice to serve

Begin by marinating tempeh strips in 1 tablespoon tamari sauce, 2 cloves minced garlic, and 1 teaspoon minced ginger. This can be done just before cooking if necessary. Sauté scallions, remaining ginger, and remaining garlic in oil in a wok over medium-low heat. Add in one vegetable at a time and stir-fry each for 30 to 60 seconds on the bottom of the wok. Cook carrots first, then push them off to the sides; sauté celery, then broccoli. As more food is added to wok, slowly increase heat to high. If more liquid is needed at any time during cooking, add a few tablespoons water. Place tempeh in bottom of wok and stir-fry for 5 minutes. Add and sauté green pepper, then red pepper. Evenly distribute 2 tablespoons tamari over the whole mixture. Cover and let steam for 1 minute (if water is needed, add ⅛ cup). Serve over brown rice.

Nutrition information per serving (without the rice): calories: 170, fat: 10 g, saturated fat: 0 g, total carbs: 10 g, fiber: 6 g, sodium: 350 mg, protein: 8 g

Desserts

Delicious indulgences can be guilt-free. The bottom line with desserts is that they should be considered treats—they should be indulged in only once in a while and in moderate portions. The healthiest dessert is fresh fruit by itself or topped with low-fat or fat-free yogurt. Healthy substitutions that can be made in dessert recipes include the following.

Instead of	Use
Whole milk	1% milk or soy milk
Cream	Fat-free half-and-half
Butter or shortening/lard	Canola oil or trans fat–free margarine
White flour	Mixture of white and whole-wheat flour
Sugar	Dried fruit or fresh fruit puree, or less sugar
Eggs	Egg substitute
Whipped cream	Fat-free whipped cream
Chocolate chips	Semisweet or dark chocolate chips or carob chips
Sour cream	Low-fat or fat-free yogurt
Custard or cream fillings	Silken tofu blended with flavorings
Regular pie crust	Reduced-fat and whole-wheat pie crusts

Yogurt Cheesecake

Makes 10–12 servings

4 cups Yogurt "Cheese" (see "Appetizers and Snacks")
2 cups sugar
1½ cup egg substitute
1 tablespoon fresh lemon juice
1 teaspoon grated fresh lemon peel (zest)
1 teaspoon vanilla extract
3 tablespoons sifted cake flour

Preheat oven to 325°F. Spray the sides and bottom of a 2-quart baking dish with nonstick cooking spray. Whip yogurt cheese with sugar, egg substitute, lemon juice, lemon peel, vanilla, and cake flour until the ingredients have been well incorporated and there are no lumps in the batter; do not overbeat. Pour into prepared dish and set in a large pan of hot (not boiling) water. Bake for 90 minutes or until cake is lightly browned and cracked. Turn oven off and leave cake in oven for 1 hour longer. Remove cheesecake from water bath and allow to cool in dish on a wire rack for 1 hour. Place serving platter over dish and invert. Chill until ready to serve. Serve topped with fresh fruit.

Nutrition information per serving: calories: 325, fat: 1 g, saturated fat: 0 g, total carbs: 65 g, fiber: 0 g, sodium: 180 mg, protein: 14 g

Chocolate-Raspberry Pie

Makes 8 servings

1 cup low-fat, no-added-salt cottage cheese
¾ cup skim milk
⅓ cup raspberry "spreadable" fruit
1 1-ounce package instant, sugar-free chocolate pudding
1 1-ounce carton frozen, fat-free nondairy whipped topping,
  thawed
Chocolate syrup
½ cup unsweetened raspberries

In a blender, combine cottage cheese, milk, and spreadable fruit. Cover and blend until smooth. Add pudding mix; mix well. Pour into bowl. Fold in whipped topping. Spoon into a 9-inch pie plate. Drizzle with syrup. Cover and freeze for 8 hours. Let stand at room temperature for 20 minutes before serving. Garnish with fresh raspberries.

Nutrition information per serving: calories: 120, fat: 0.5 g, saturated fat: 0.5 g, total carbs: 25 g, fiber: 0 g, sodium: 75 mg, protein: 5 g

Apple-Cranberry Crisp

Makes 10–12 ½-cup servings

1 12-ounce package cranberries

2 large apples, peeled, cored, and sliced thin

½ cup sugar

1 teaspoon cinnamon

¼ cup unbleached or whole-wheat flour, divided

2 tablespoons packed brown sugar

¾ cup old-fashioned oats

½ cup chopped walnuts

3 tablespoons trans fat–free margarine, melted

Preheat oven to 375°F. In a large bowl, combine cranberries, apples, sugar, cinnamon, and 1 tablespoon flour. Transfer the mixture to a greased, 6-cup, shallow baking dish. In the same bowl (no need to wash it), combine remaining flour, brown sugar, oats, and nuts. Stir in the melted butter and mix well (the mixture should be crumbly). Sprinkle oat mixture over fruit mixture. Bake for 40 minutes, or until the crisp is lightly browned. Let stand for 10 minutes before serving.

Nutrition information per serving: calories: 175, fat: 6 g, saturated fat: 0 g, total carbs: 28 g, fiber: 0 g, sodium: 20 mg, protein: 2.5 g

Double Ginger Cookies

Makes approximately 24 cookies

1½ cups all-purpose flour

1 cup whole-wheat flour

¾ cup chopped crystallized ginger

½ teaspoon ground ginger

1 teaspoon baking powder

½ teaspoon baking soda

¼ teaspoon salt

1¼ cups sugar, divided

½ cup unsweetened applesauce

¼ cup canola oil

1 teaspoon grated lemon rind

1 tablespoon lemon juice

¼ teaspoon vanilla extract

Combine both flours, chopped and ground ginger, baking powder, baking soda, and salt; stir well with a whisk. Make a well in center of mixture. Combine 1 cup sugar and remaining ingredients. Add to flour mixture, stirring just until moist. Cover and chill for 1 to 24 hours.

Preheat oven to 350°F. Flour hands and shape dough into 24 balls (2 tablespoons each). Roll balls in ¼ cup sugar. Spray a cookie sheet with nonstick cooking spray; place balls 2 inches apart on cookie sheet. Press to flatten slightly. Bake for 15 minutes, or until lightly browned.

Nutrition information per serving (2 cookies): calories: 215, fat: 5 g, saturated fat: 0 g, total carbs: 40 g, fiber: 1 g, sodium: 120 mg, protein: 3 g

Healthy Granola Balls ✓

Makes approximately 24 balls

  1 cup soy granola (or any fat-free granola)
  1 cup high-fiber breakfast cereal
  ¼ cup dried fruit (raisins, cranberries, pineapple chunks,
    and so on)
  ½ cup miniature marshmallows
  2 tablespoons honey
  2 tablespoons natural unsalted peanut butter

Line a baking sheet with waxed paper. Mix granola, cereal, and dried fruit in a medium bowl. Heat remaining ingredients in a small nonstick saucepan over low heat, stirring constantly. Immediately after melting the marshmallows, pour over cereal mixture and stir until coated evenly. Using wet hands, shape into 1½-inch balls, then place on waxed paper. Refrigerate for 30 minutes or until set.

Nutrition information per serving (2 balls): calories: 100, fat: 2 g, saturated fat: 0 g, total carbs: 15 g, fiber: 5 g, sodium: 50 mg, protein: 5 g

Tofu Pumpkin Pie

Makes 8 servings

1 10.5-ounce package soft or silken tofu
1 15-ounce can pumpkin puree
½ cup sugar
2 teaspoons pumpkin pie spice
1 frozen whole-wheat pie crust

Preheat oven to 425°F. Drain tofu well, then puree in a blender until smooth. In a mixing bowl, whisk together pumpkin and sugar. Whisk in spice and pureed tofu. Pour mixture into thawed pie shell and bake for 15 minutes. Lower heat to 350°F, and bake for an additional 40 minutes. Chill before cutting into eighths and serving.

Nutrition information per serving: calories: 235, fat: 8 g, saturated fat: 1 g, total carbs: 37 g, fiber: 1.5 g, sodium: 21 mg, protein: 5 g

Appendi..

Healthy Grocery Shopping List

Meal planning can make healthy eating easy by reducing impulse buying and snacking. Planning meals for a week and putting together a healthy grocery shopping list can simplify heart-healthy cooking and eating. This list contains examples of food items from the different components of a balanced plate—whole grains, lean protein, vegetables, and fruit. It also contains examples of healthy, low-sodium seasonings and condiments, as well as desserts and snacks. This shopping list can be used as a reference to stock up your pantry and refrigerator with heart-healthy ingredients.

Whole Grains and High-Fiber Starches

- Whole-wheat bread (at least 2 grams of fiber per serving)
- Whole-wheat pita bread
- Whole-wheat bagels/muffins
- Whole-grain crackers (at least 2 grams of fiber per serving)
- Brown rice, instant brown rice
- Quinoa
- Whole-wheat couscous
- Whole-wheat pasta
- Whole-grain breakfast cereals (at least 5 grams of fiber per serving)
- Oatmeal
- Bulgur
- Sweet potatoes/yams
- Winter squashes (acorn, butternut, and blue Hubbard)

Green peas
- Corn

Fruits and Vegetables
- Fresh fruit and vegetables, especially darker colored ones such as spinach, romaine lettuce, berries, melons, peppers, and broccoli
- Prewashed salad mixes and baby spinach
- Frozen vegetables such as spinach, carrots, broccoli, and green beans

Protein
- White-meat chicken and turkey
- Skinless ground turkey and chicken
- Precooked grilled chicken strips
- Low-sodium, low-fat deli turkey/chicken/ham
- Fish—especially oily fish such as salmon, mackerel, bluefish, swordfish, trout, sardines, and herring
- Round and loin cuts of red meat (occasionally)
- Pork tenderloin
- Veggie burgers
- Tofu, marinated or smoked
- Tempeh
- Soy crumbles (to replace ground beef)
- Low-fat, low-sodium cheese
- Low-fat milk, skim milk, soy milk
- Low-fat/fat-free yogurt and cottage cheese
- Yogurt cheese (Make your own from fat-free plain yogurt.)
- Canned beans (rinsed to remove excess sodium)
- Lentils
- Hummus
- Natural, unsalted peanut butter, almond butter, soy nut butter
- Unsalted nuts
- Egg substitute
- Eggs (in moderation)

Low-Sodium Seasonings and Condiments

- Olive oil, canola oil
- Vinegars
- Lime juice, lemon juice
- Tabasco sauce
- Low-sodium salsa
- Mrs. Dash (sodium-free) 10-Minute marinades
- Trans fat–free margarine
- Herbox (low-sodium) bouillon
- Mustard
- Pepper, lemon pepper
- Garlic, ginger
- Other spices and herbs

Desserts and Snacks

- Dried fruit
- Trail mix (Make your own with high-fiber cereal, nuts, and dried fruit.)
- Fat-free/low-fat flavored yogurt
- Fat-free/low-fat frozen yogurt
- Graham crackers
- Vanilla wafers
- Angel food cake
- Fat-free instant Jell-O and Jell-O pudding
- Soy chips

Glossary

adrenaline and noradrenaline: Also called *epinephrine* and *norepinephrine*, these key stress hormones cause a cascade of physiological responses in the body, such as faster heartbeat and respiration, a rise in blood pressure, and the release of energy-boosting fats and glucose.

aldosterone: A hormone secreted by the adrenal glands that signals the kidneys to conserve sodium and water; the result is higher blood pressure.

angiotensin: A protein that increases blood pressure by constricting blood vessels and stimulating the release of aldosterone. The inactive form is angiotensin I, and the active form is angiotensin II.

antihypertensives: Medications used to treat high blood pressure.

arterial resistance: The pressure that artery walls exert on blood flow; in general, the less elastic the arteries, the greater the arterial resistance and the higher the blood pressure.

atherosclerosis: A thickening of the inner layer of artery walls from the buildup of debris, such as fats and cholesterol, from the bloodstream; this narrows the passageway and diminishes blood flow.

autonomic nervous system: The part of the nervous system that controls involuntary processes, such as heartbeat and breathing. Its two arms are the sympathetic and parasympathetic nervous systems.

breath focus: A form of meditation that elicits the relaxation response. Breath focus relies on deep, even breathing; a passive attitude; and a focus word or phrase.

coronary artery disease: Narrowing or blockage of the arteries that supply blood to the heart muscle. The condition can cause angina and heart attack.

cortisol: One of a class of stress hormones called *glucocorticoids*, which are released by the adrenal glands during the stress response.

diabetes: A disorder in which blood glucose (sugar) levels are elevated.

diastolic pressure: The second (bottom) reading of a blood pressure measurement, which reflects the pressure in the arteries between heartbeats.

epinephrine: A chemical released by the sympathetic nervous system that constricts blood vessels and increases heart rate; also called *adrenaline*.

focus words: Words or phrases that enhance your sense of peace, relaxation, and connection while you are practicing deep breathing and other techniques that elicit the relaxation response.

HPA (hypothalamic-pituitary-adrenal) axis: A system that governs many hormonal activities in the body, including the stress response.

heart failure: A condition in which the heart loses its ability to efficiently pump blood throughout the body.

hypothalamus: A network of nerves, located above the brain stem, that helps control the sympathetic and parasympathetic nervous systems and, through the pituitary gland, the endocrine system. It sparks the stress response by releasing the first of several chemical messengers that put the body on alert.

isolated systolic hypertension: A form of hypertension characterized by elevated systolic blood pressure and normal diastolic pressure.

labile hypertension: Blood pressure that frequently fluctuates between normal and abnormal during the course of a day, often within only a few minutes.

left ventricular hypertrophy (LVH): Thickening of the left ventricle, the chamber of the heart that pumps blood to the body.

malignant hypertension: A dangerous type of hypertension marked by an unusually sudden rise in blood pressure to very high levels, often accompanied by headache, blurred vision, and seizures.

mindfulness: As an ancient Buddhist practice, a type of meditation that induces the relaxation response by focusing your mind on the distracting thoughts and sensations that may occur during meditation. Also refers to nonmeditative techniques that encourage you to slow your pace and live fully in the moment.

neurotransmitters: Chemicals released by nerve cells that transmit messages to other nearby cells.

norepinephrine: A neurotransmitter that constricts blood vessels.

parasympathetic nervous system: One of two offshoots of the autonomic nervous system, the parasympathetic nervous system calms body systems excited by the release of stress hormones.

post-traumatic stress disorder (PTSD): A prolonged reaction to trauma characterized by recurrent flashbacks, dreams, or intrusive thoughts about the traumatic event; withdrawal from people and certain situations; edginess; and difficulty sleeping.

primary hypertension: High blood pressure for which there is no known underlying cause; also called *essential hypertension*.

progressive muscle relaxation (PMR): A tool for inducing the relaxation response. PMR teaches you to isolate a specific set of muscles, tense them briefly, and then relax.

pulse pressure: The difference between your systolic and diastolic blood pressures, which may help predict heart disease risk.

relaxation response: A term coined by Herbert Benson, M.D., to describe the physical effects of meditation and certain other techniques that counter the stress response. Effects include marked drops in oxygen consumption, carbon dioxide expiration, heartbeat, and respiration, as well as the stabilization of or a decrease in blood pressure.

renal artery stenosis: Narrowing of an artery that supplies blood to the kidney.

renin: An enzyme released by the kidney that stimulates production of angiotensin.

resistant hypertension: Blood pressure that remains persistently elevated despite drug therapy and lifestyle changes.

secondary hypertension: High blood pressure that has an identifiable, often correctable, cause.

stressors: Stressful events or circumstances that may be real or perceived threats to your equilibrium and well-being.

stress response: Physiological changes, such as quickened breathing and heartbeat, brought on by stress hormones released in response to a real or perceived threat to your safety or ability to cope. Also called the *fight-or-flight response*.

sympathetic nervous system: An offshoot of the autonomic nervous system, the sympathetic nervous system cranks up the body when stress hormones are released in response to perceived or real dangers.

systolic pressure: The first (top) number of a blood pressure measurement, which reflects pressure in the arteries when the heart contracts.

vasoconstrictors: Substances that constrict blood vessels.

vasodilators: Substances that widen blood vessels.

white–coat hypertension: Blood pressure elevations that occur in response to visits to a doctor's office.

Index

About the Authors

Aggie Casey, R.N., M.S., is a clinical nurse specialist and director of the Mind/Body Medical Institute (M/BMI) Cardiac Wellness Program and the clinical director of the Affiliate Cardiac Programs. She received her master's degree at the University of Massachusetts Graduate School of Nursing and has over twenty-five years of experience in providing cardiac care to patients in acute and outpatient settings. She has trained numerous health care professionals throughout the United States in health promotion and cardiac wellness. Casey is a researcher and an associate in medicine at Harvard Medical School. She is coauthor of *Mind Your Heart: A Mind/Body Approach to Stress Management, Exercise, and Nutrition.*

Herbert Benson, M.D., is the founder and president of the Mind/Body Medical Institute and an associate professor of medicine at Harvard Medical School. A graduate of Wesleyan University and Harvard Medical School, Dr. Benson authored the bestseller *The Relaxation Response*, as well as ten other books and more than 170 scientific publications. He is a pioneer in mind/body medicine as well as in bringing spirituality and healing into medicine. Throughout his career of more than thirty-five years, he defined the relaxation response and continues to lead teaching and research into its efficacy in counteracting the harmful effects of stress. The recipient of numerous national and international awards, Dr. Benson lectures widely about mind/body medicine and the M/BMI's work.